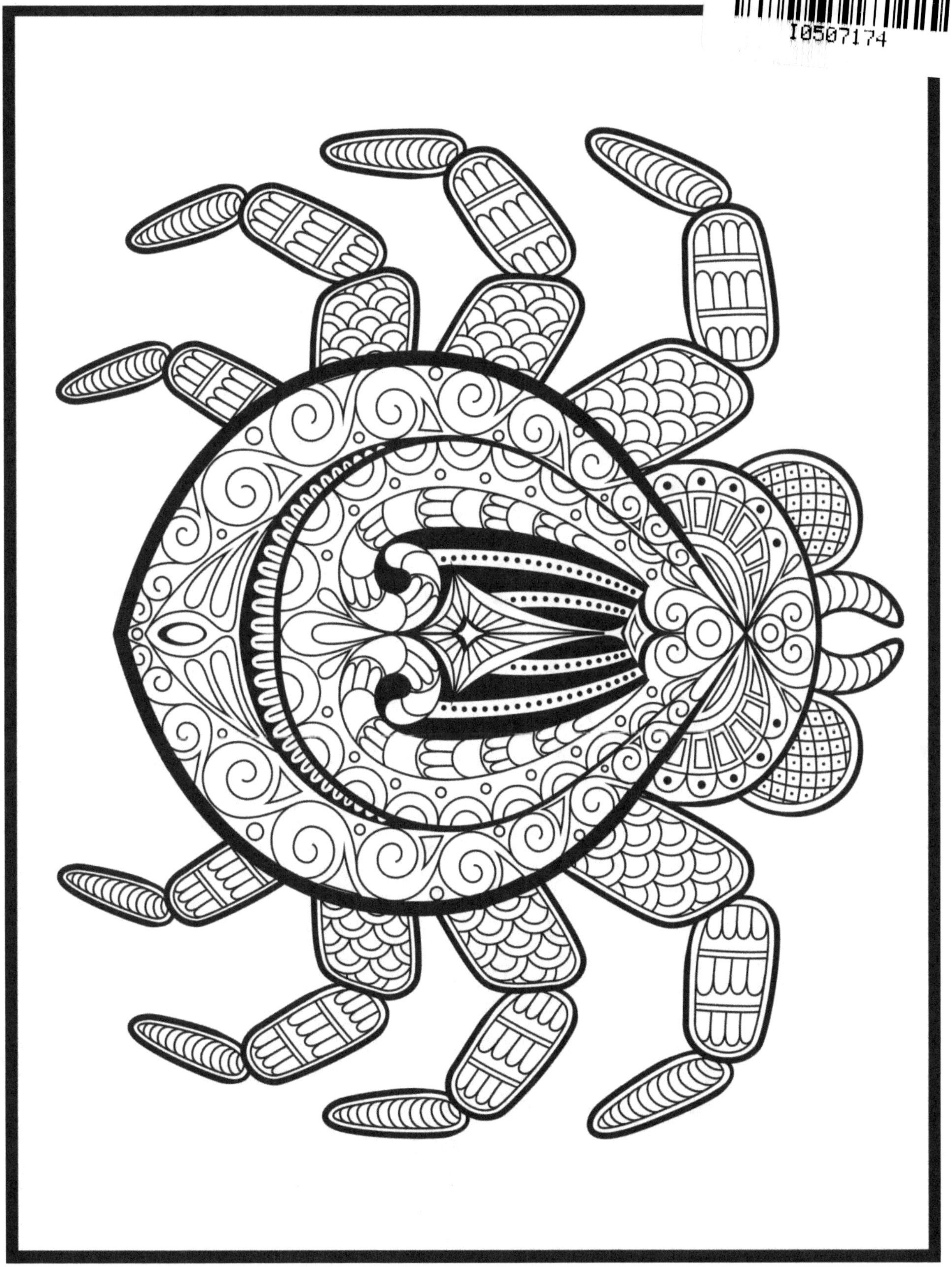

I0507174

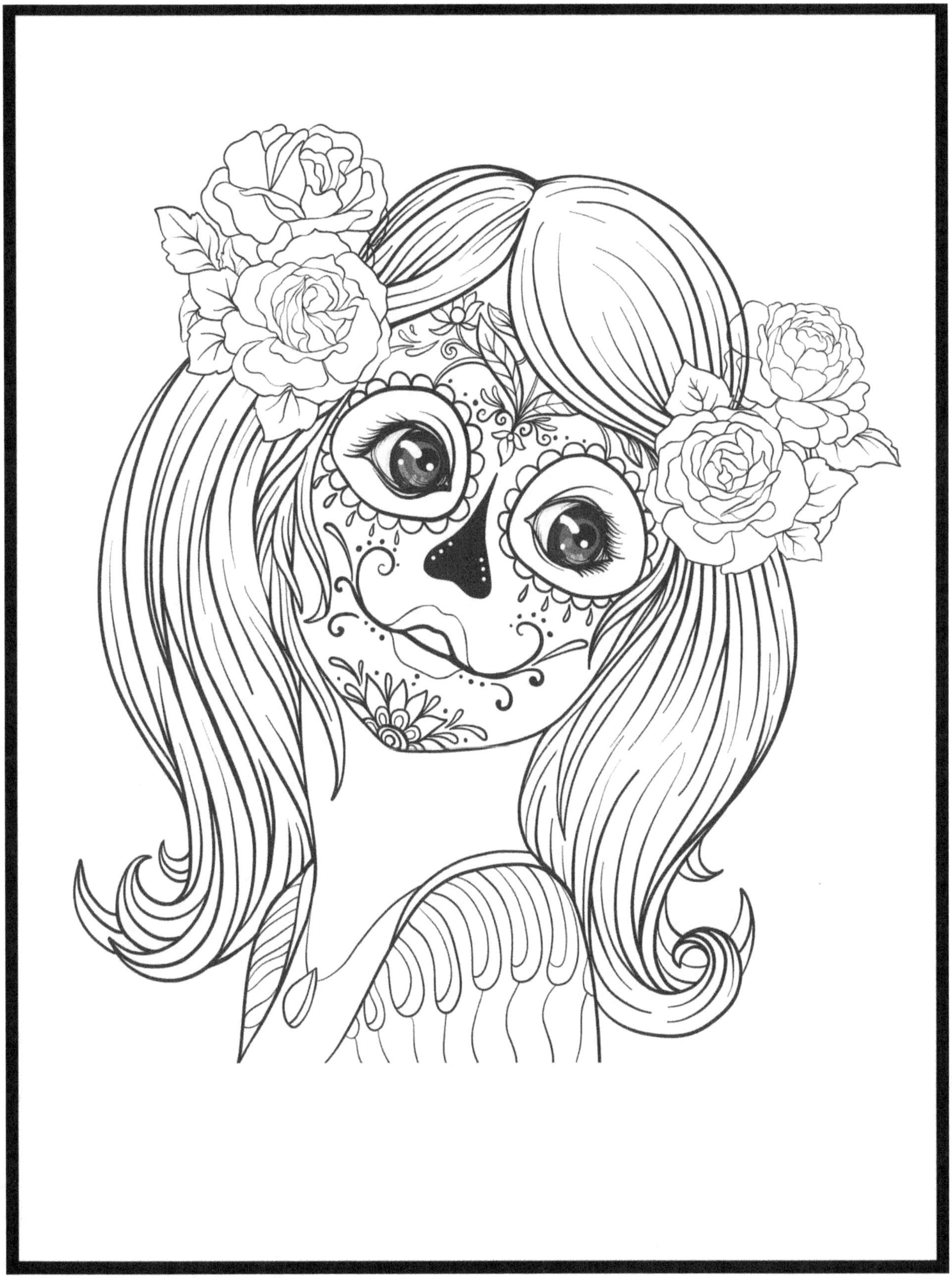

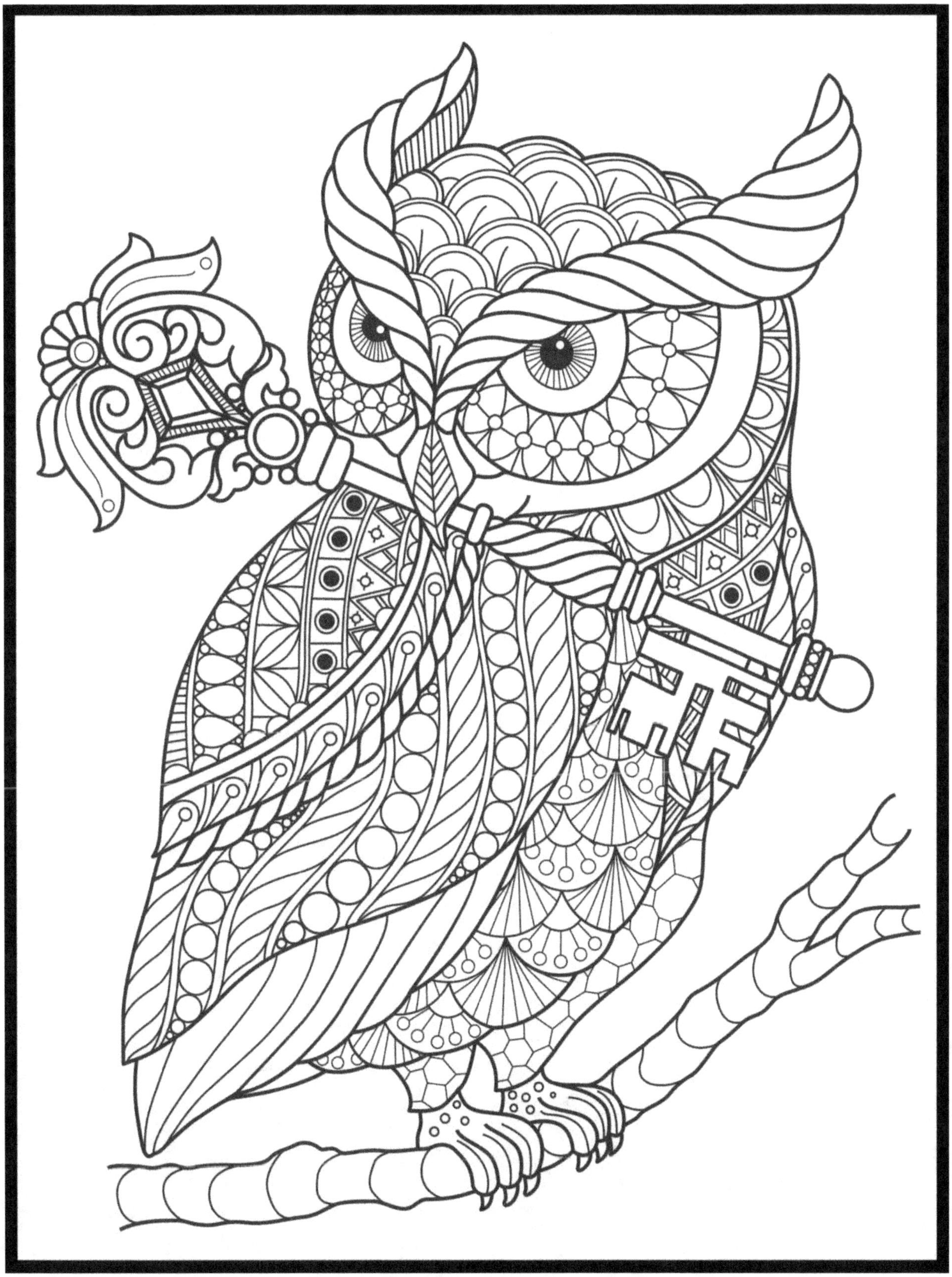

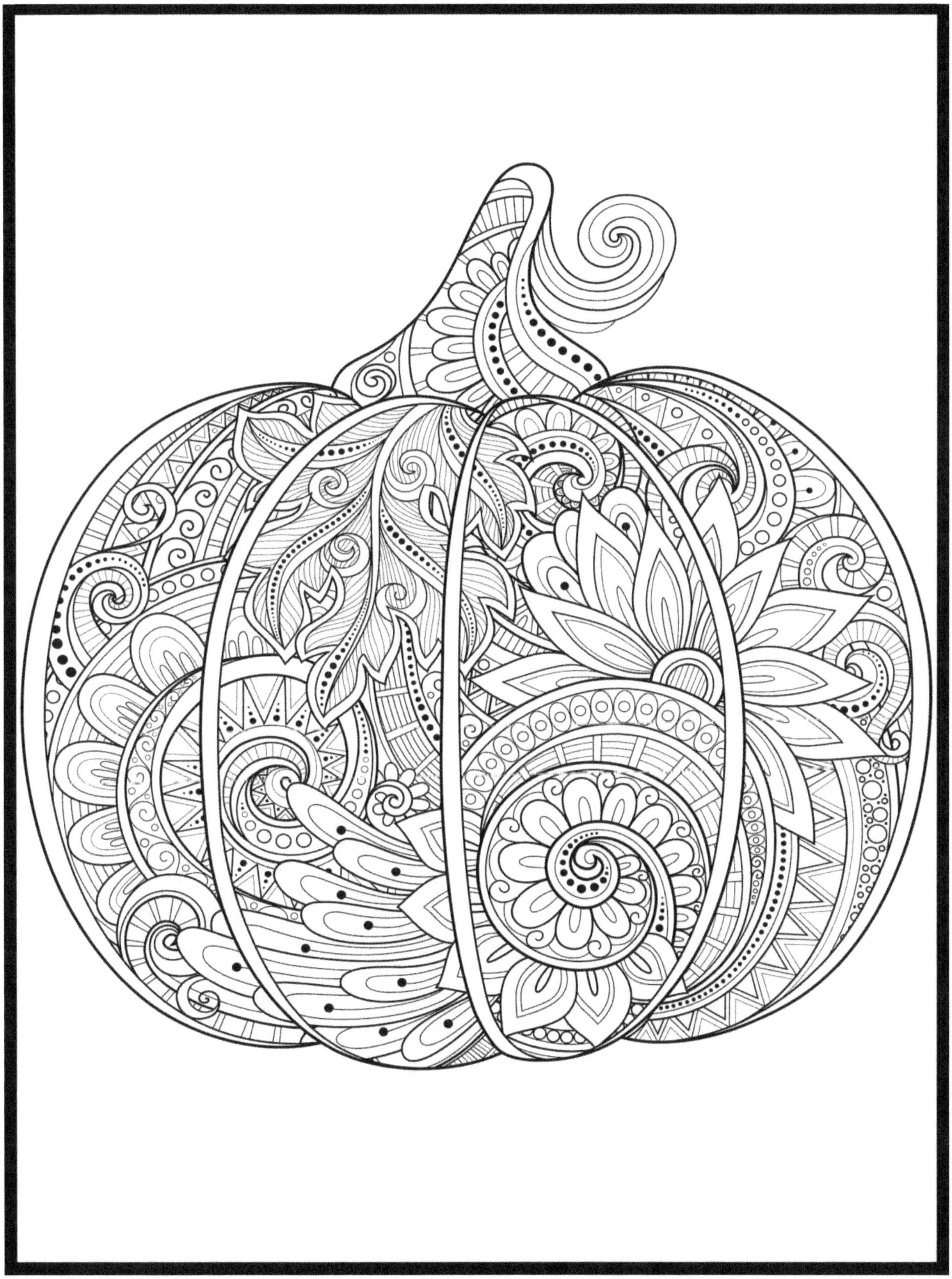

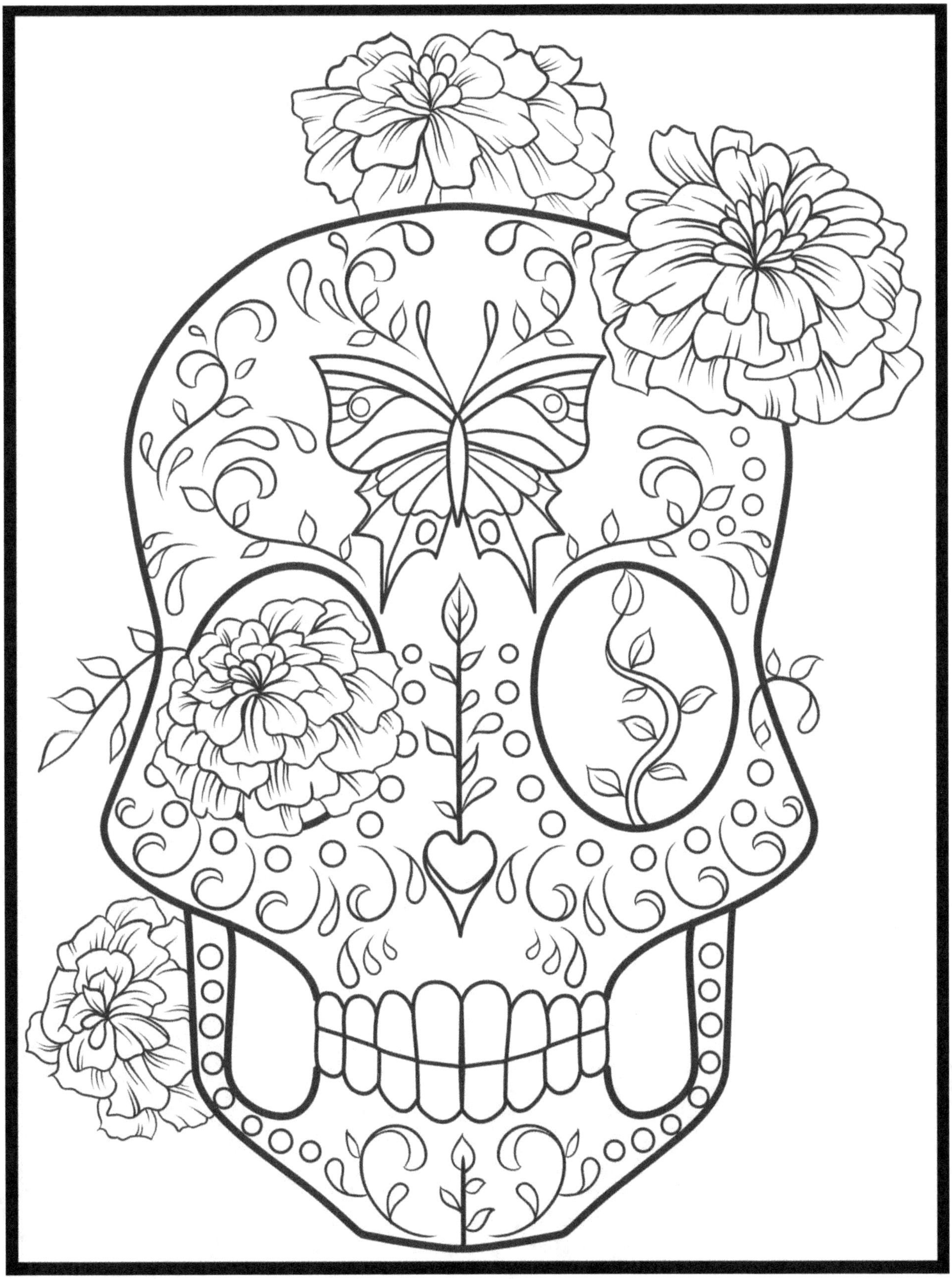

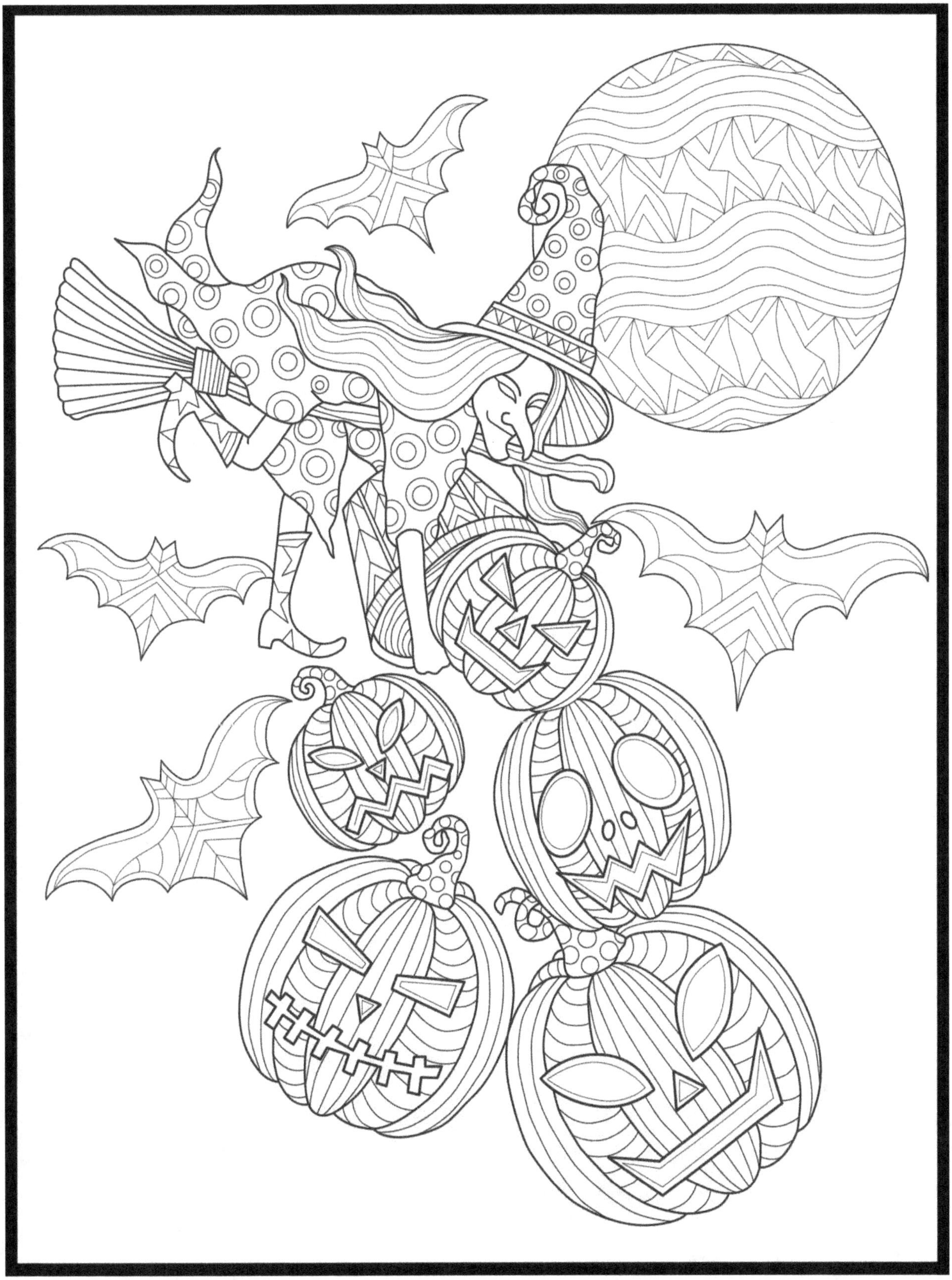

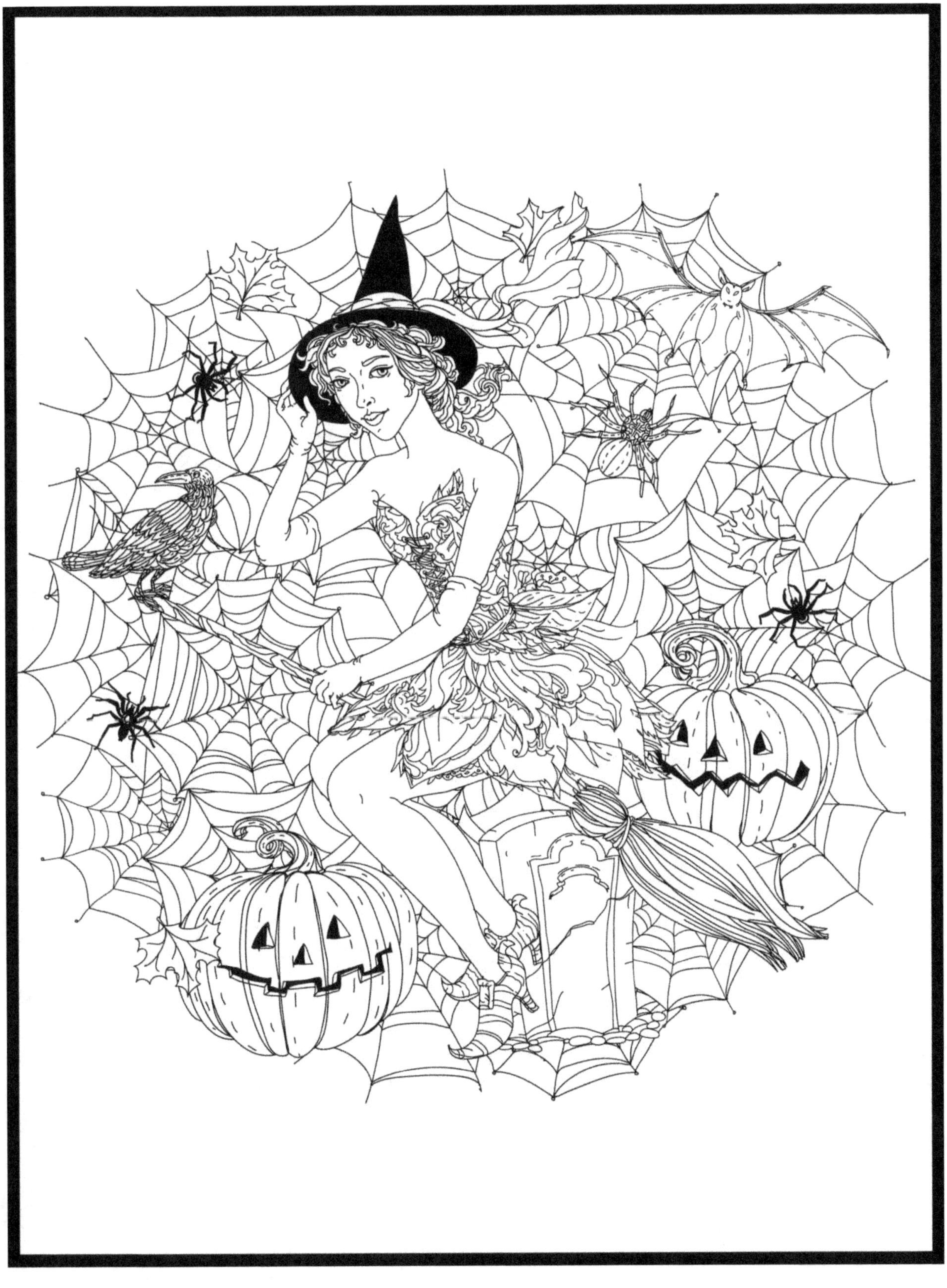

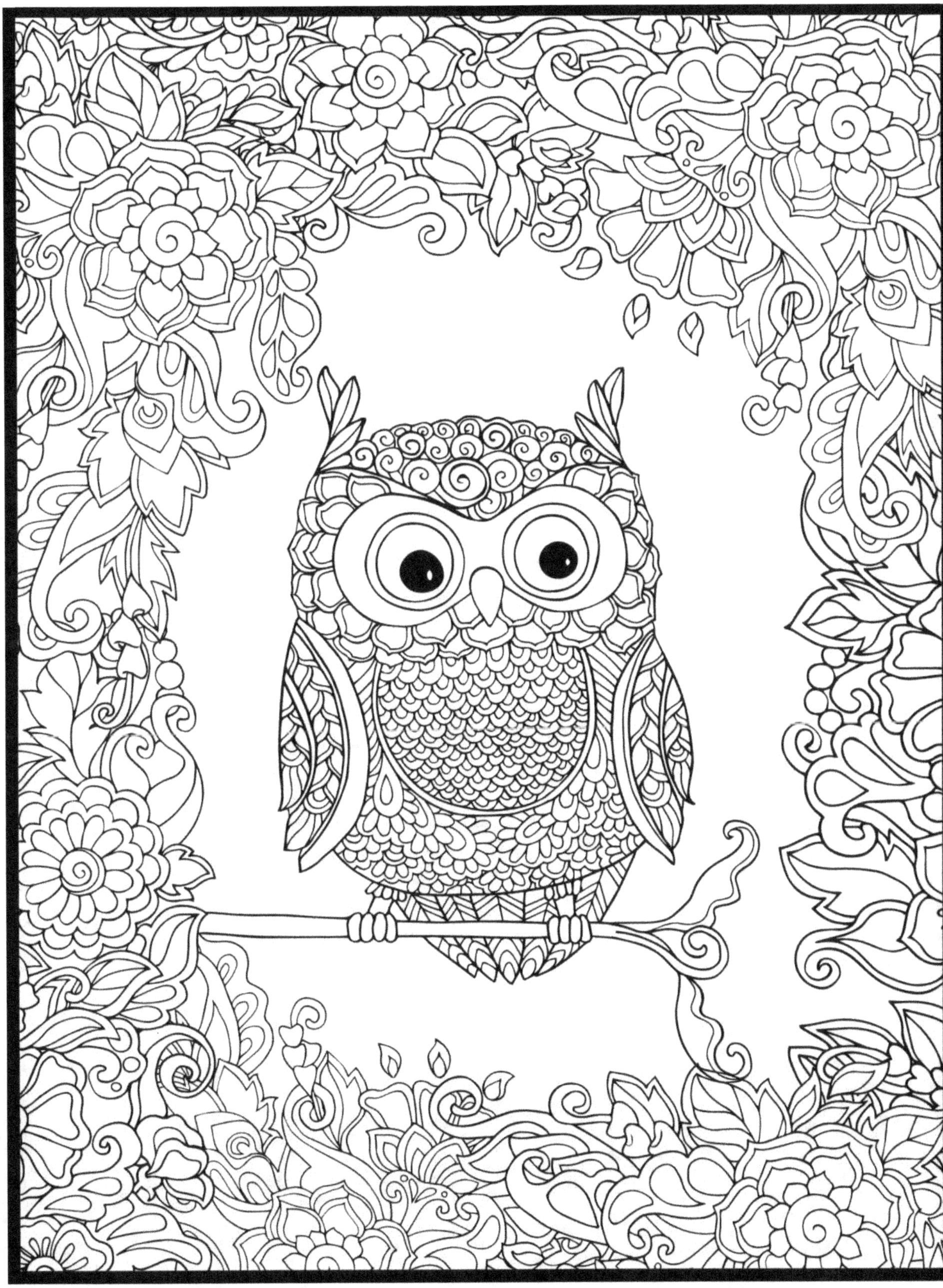

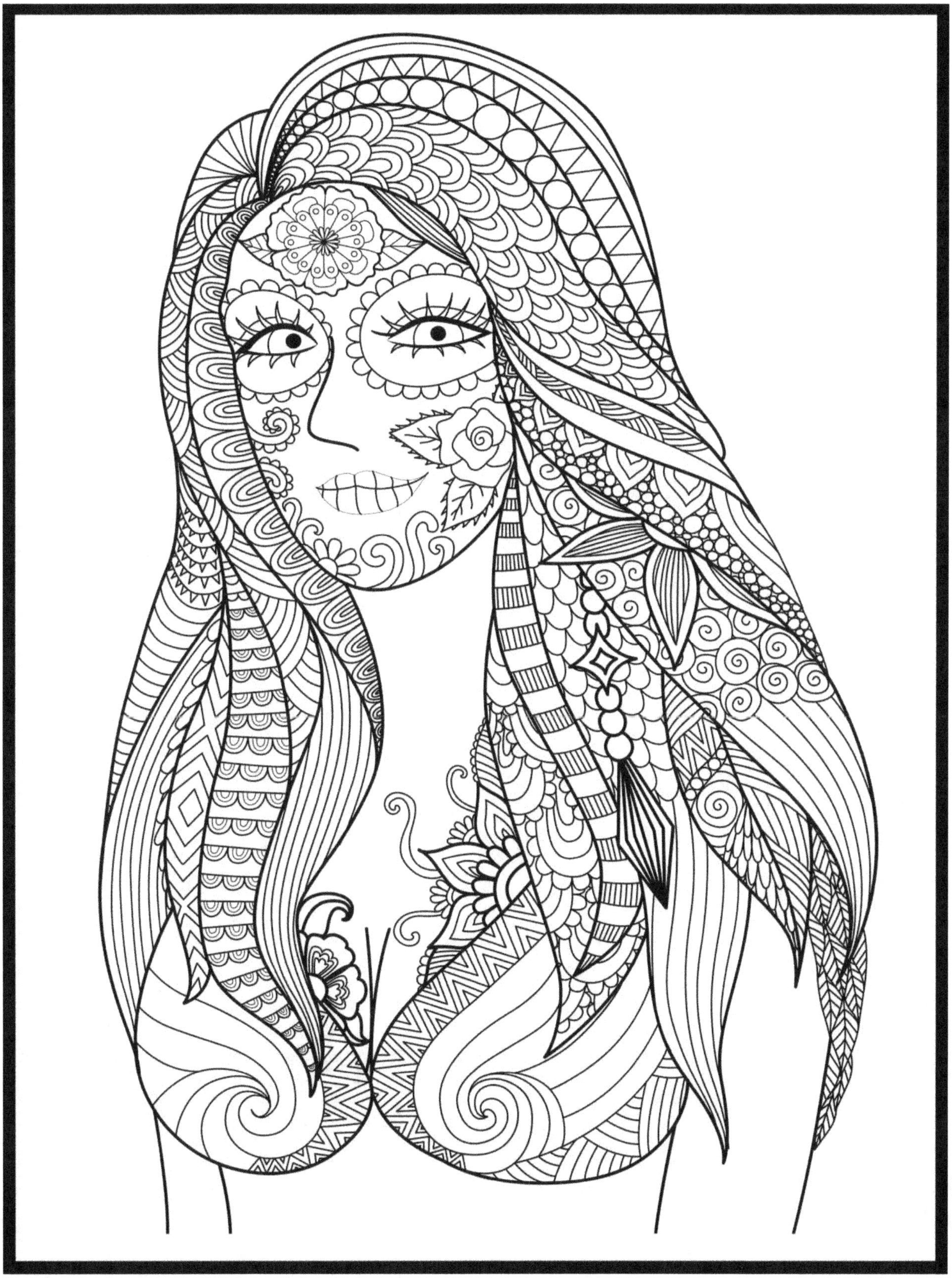

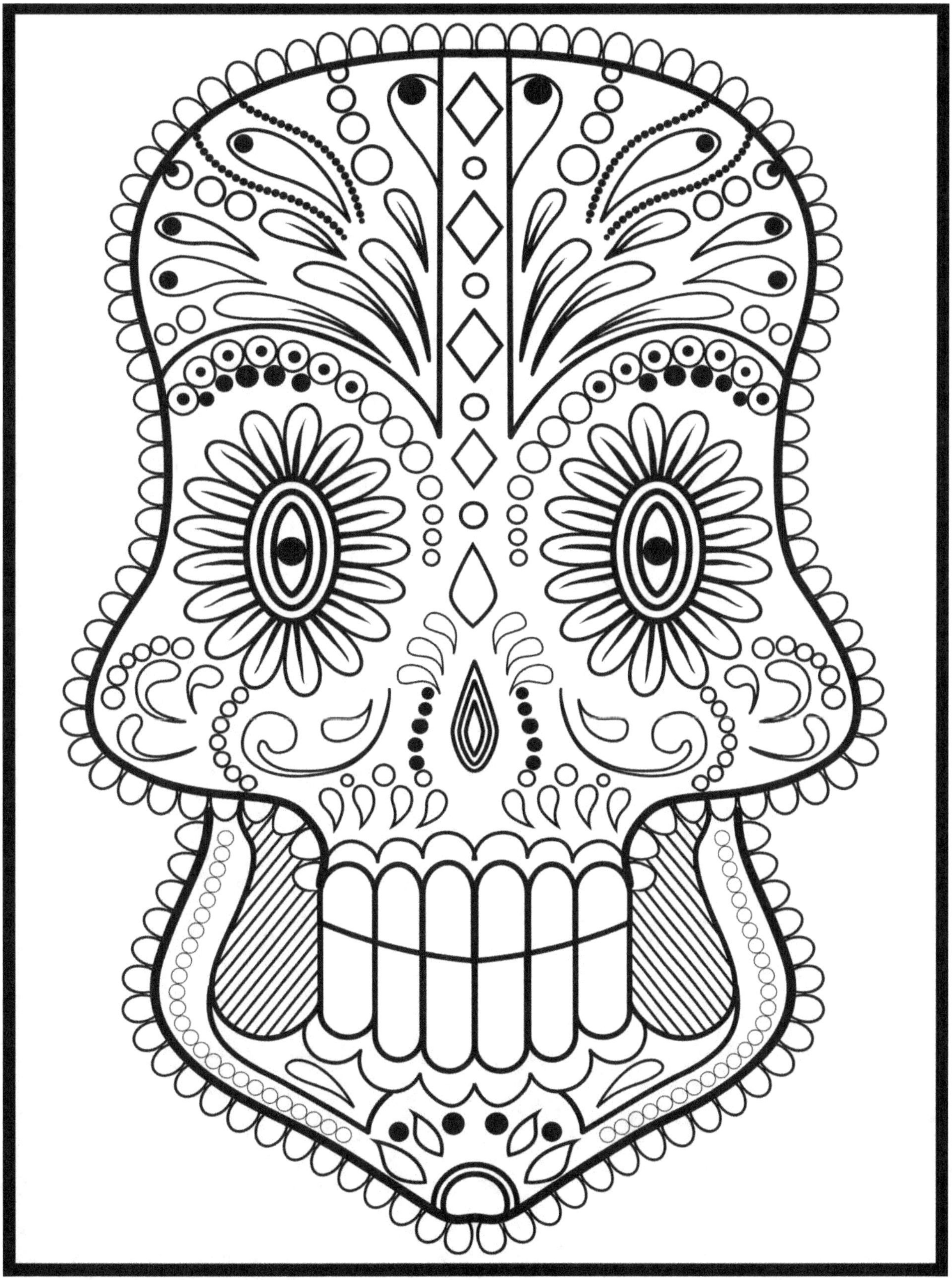

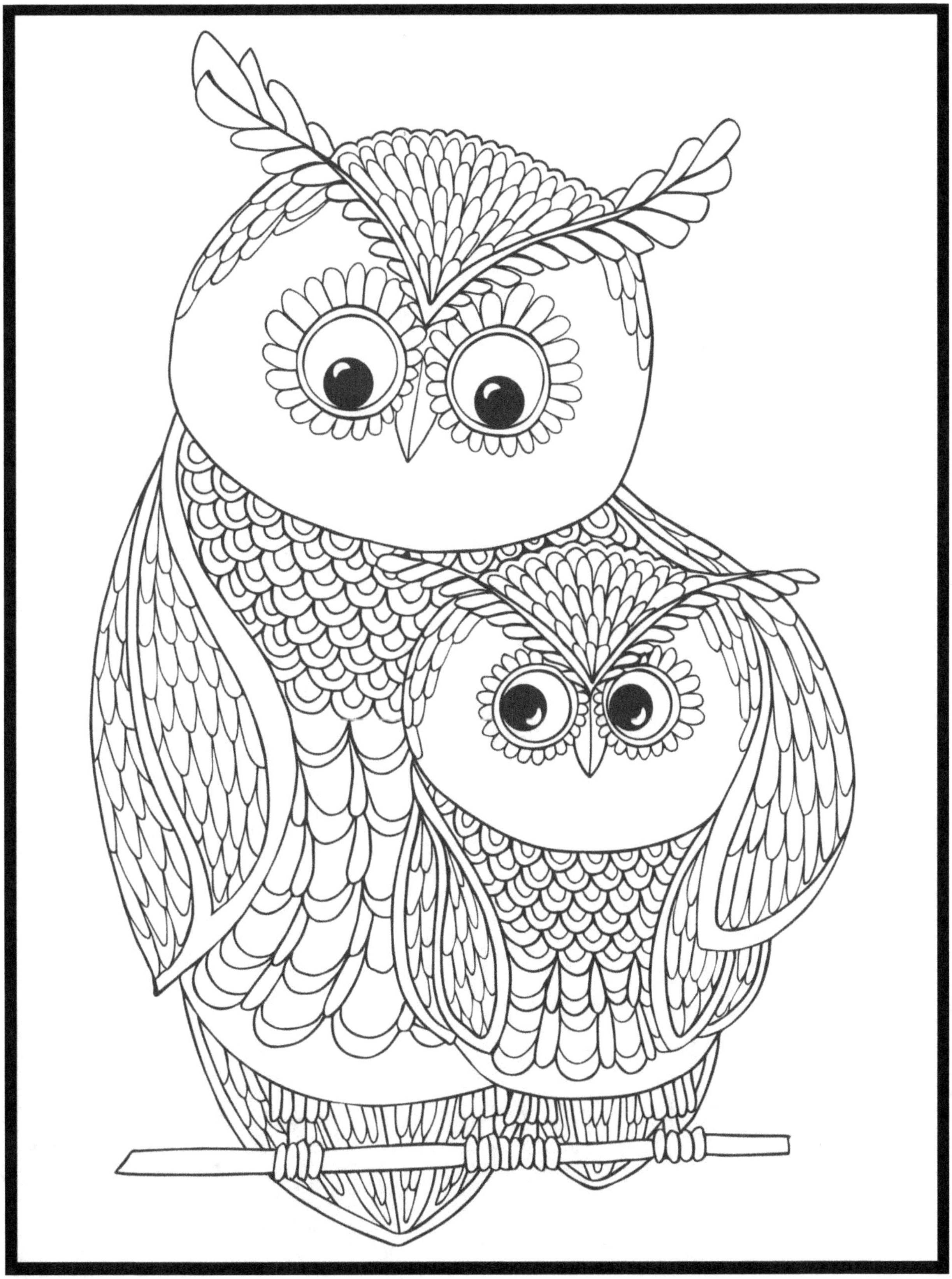

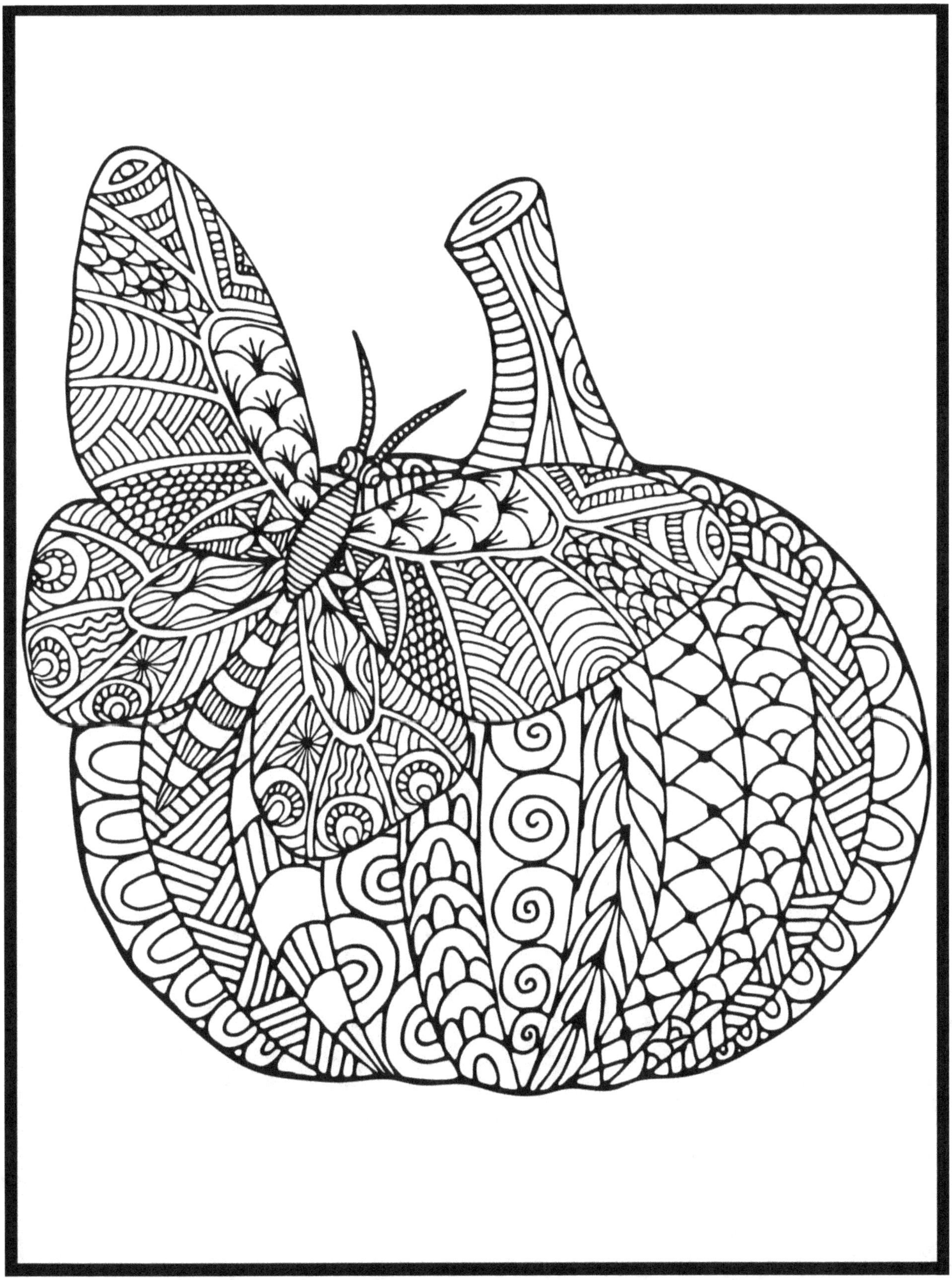

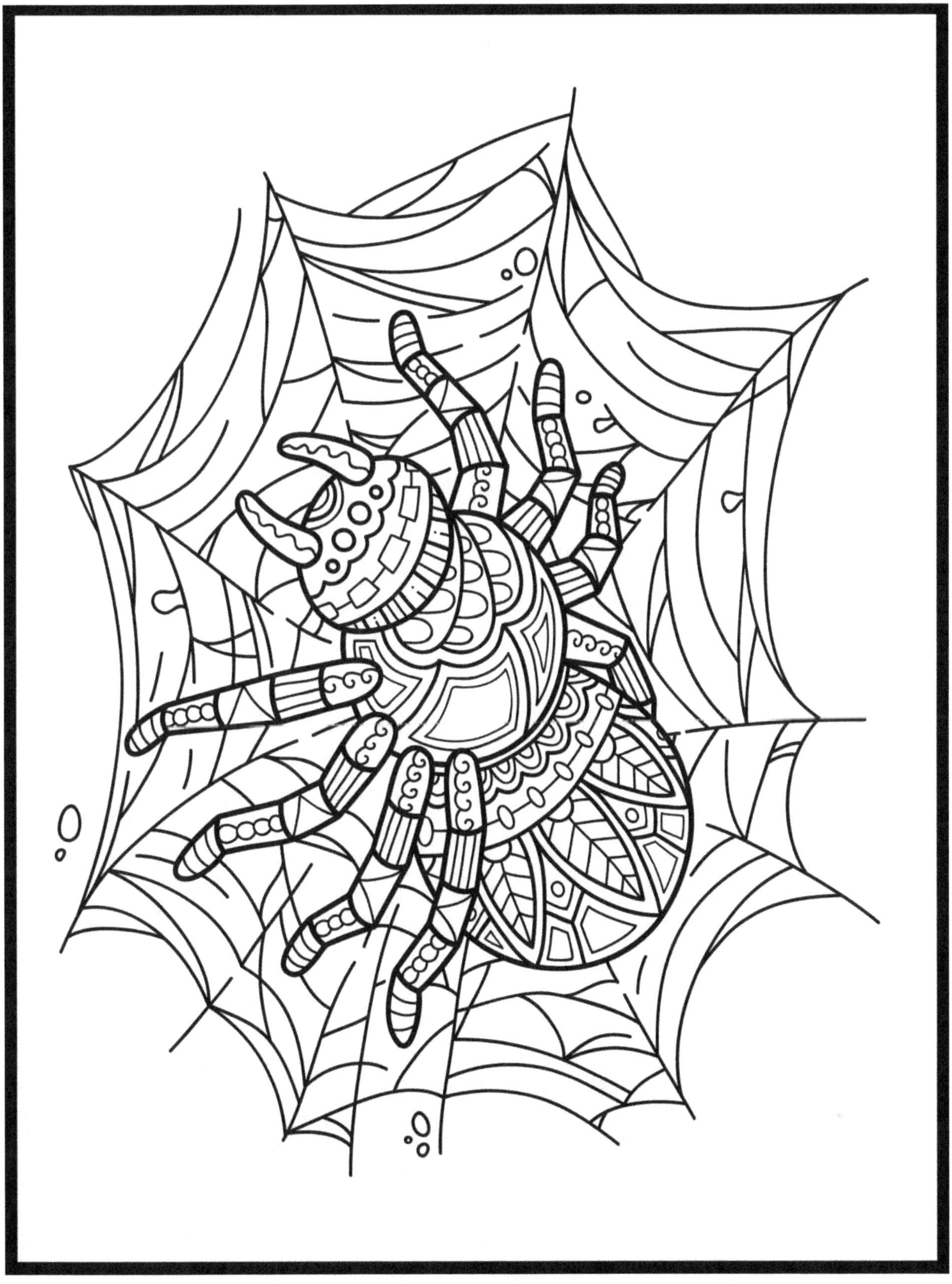

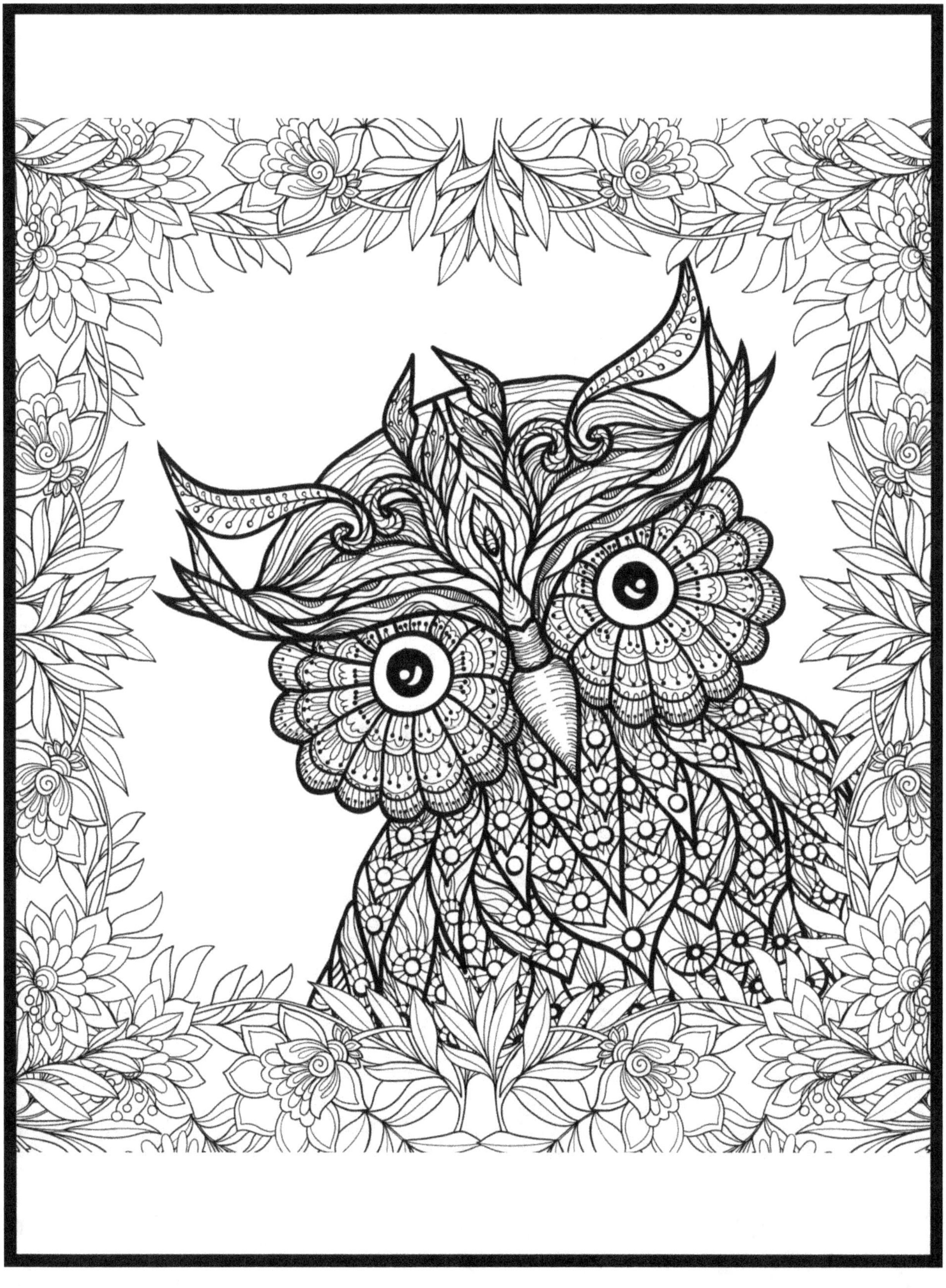

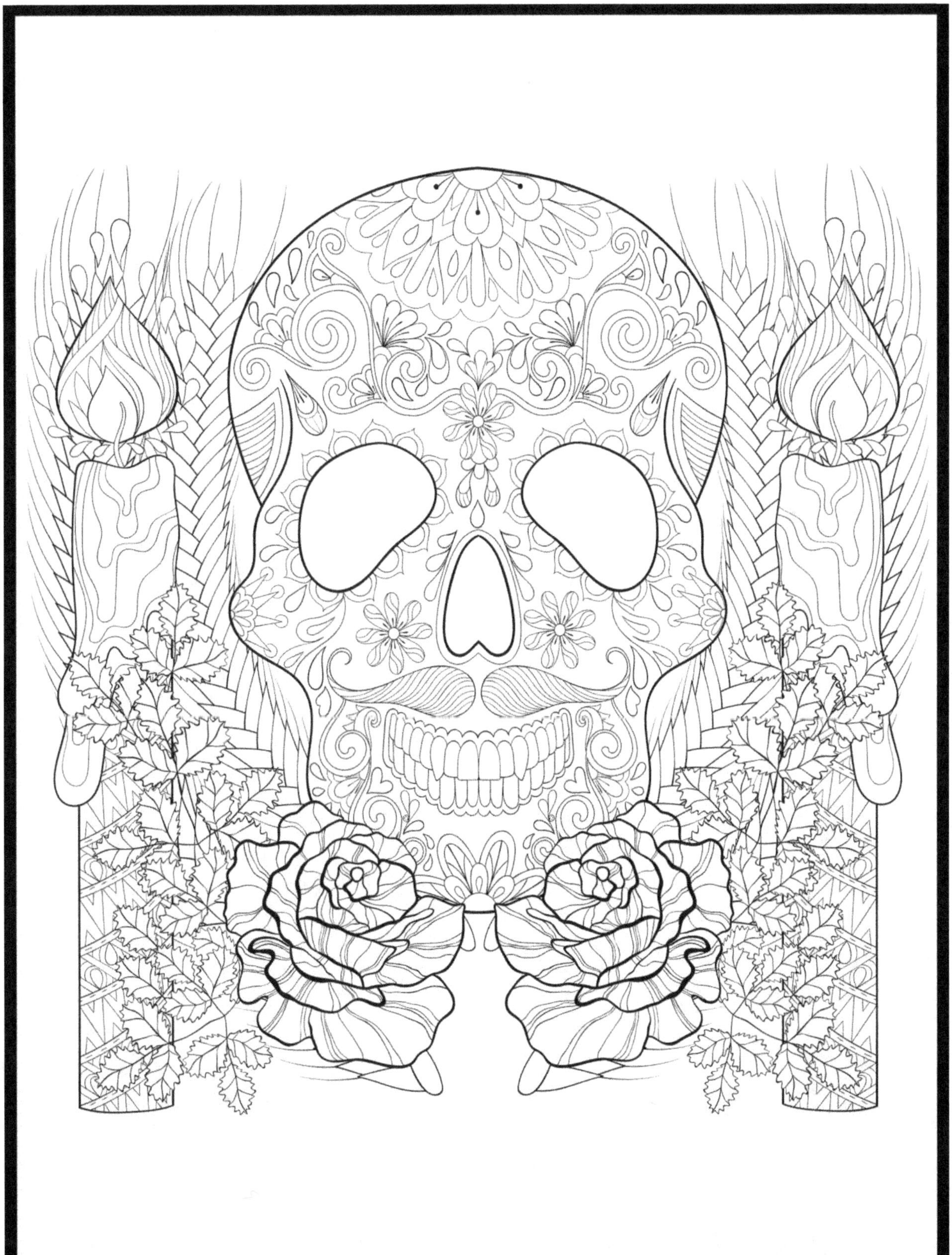

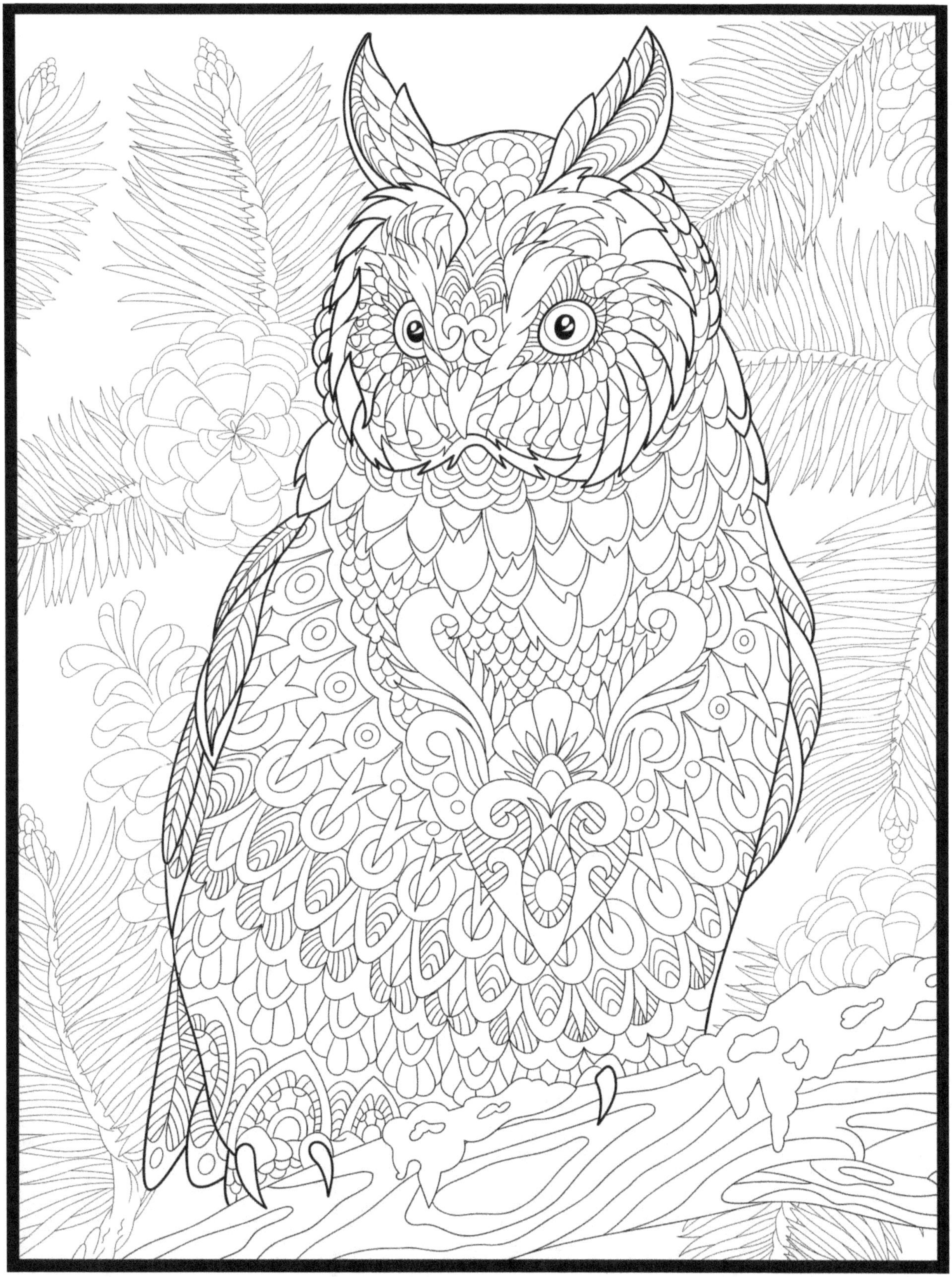

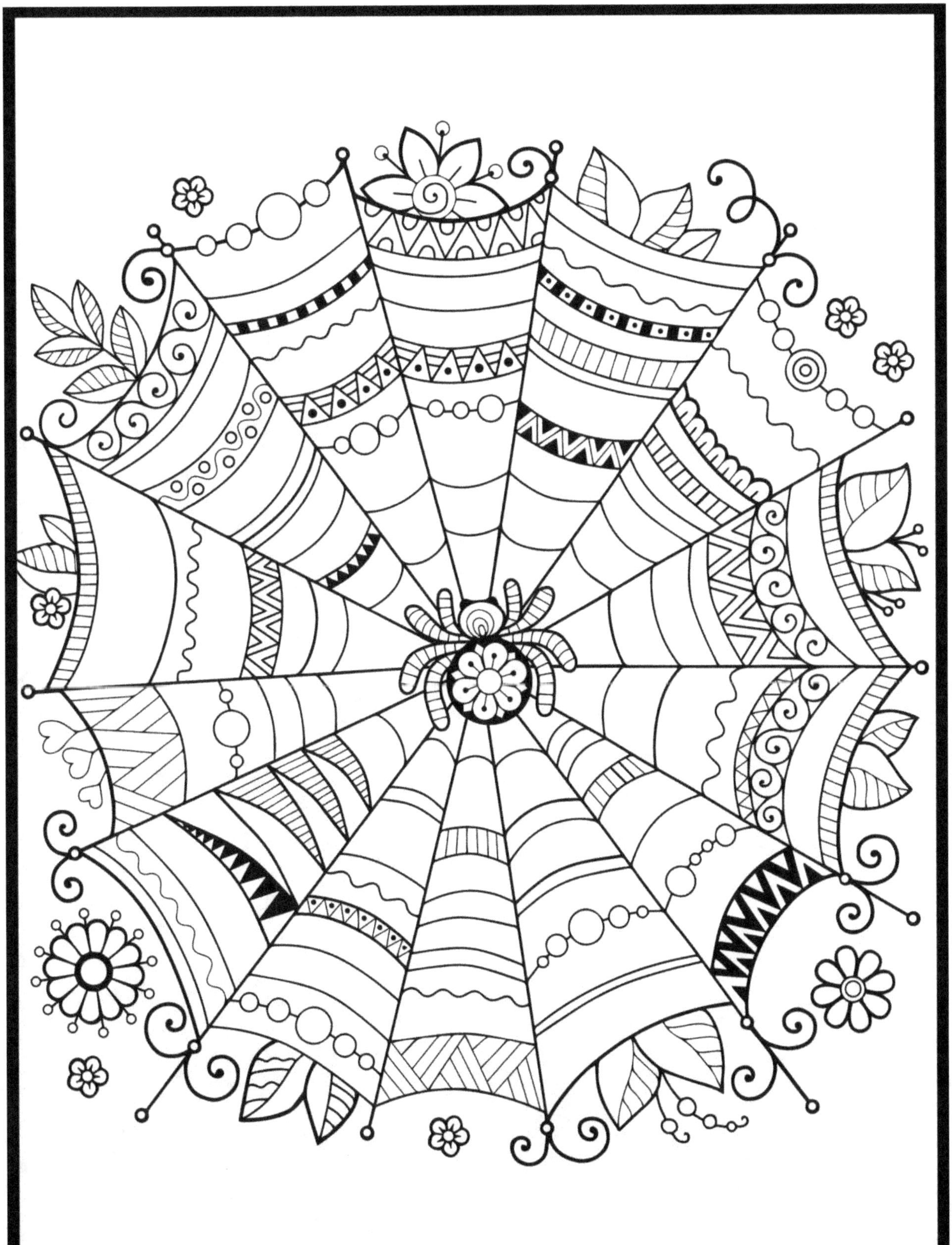

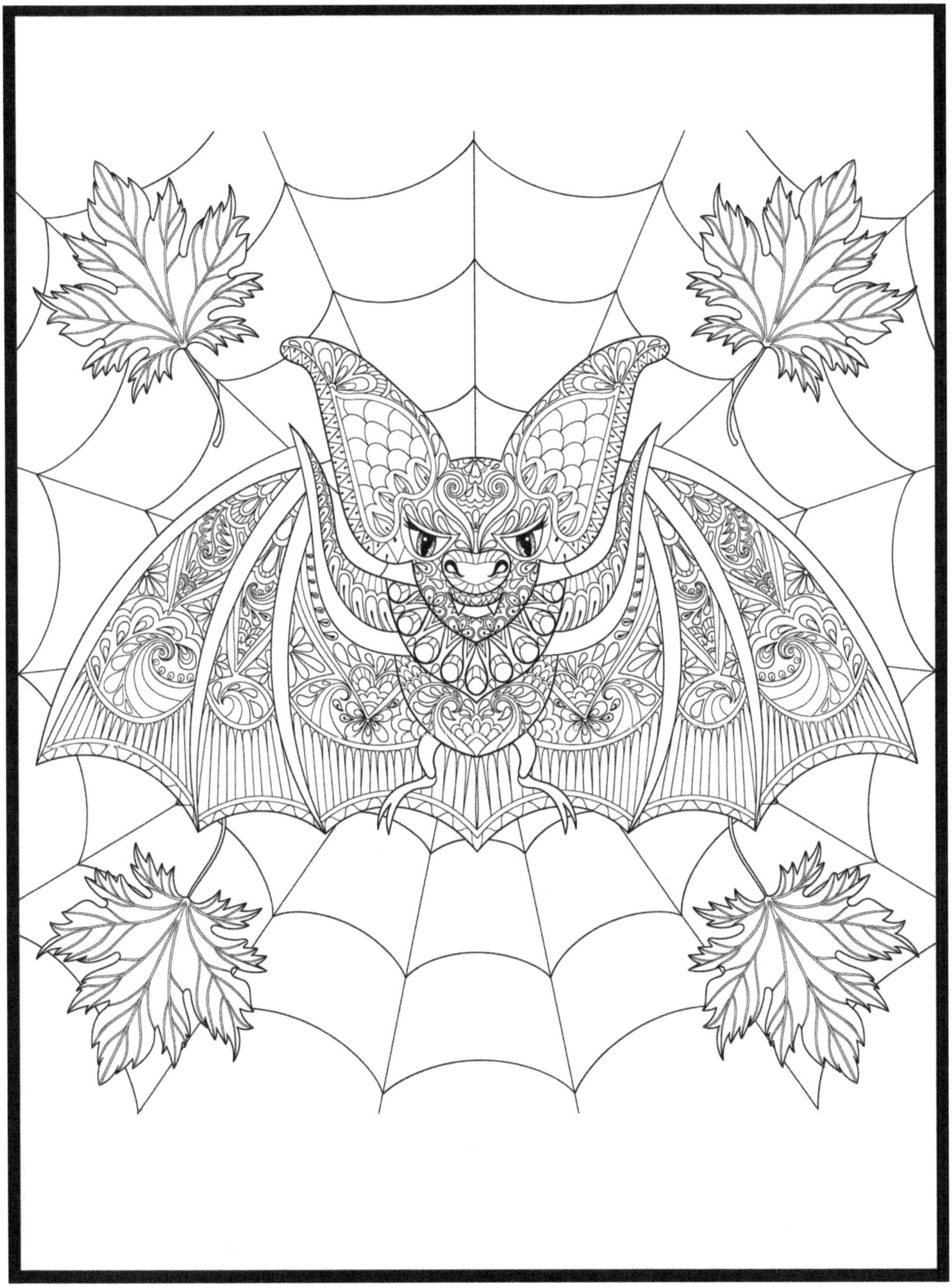

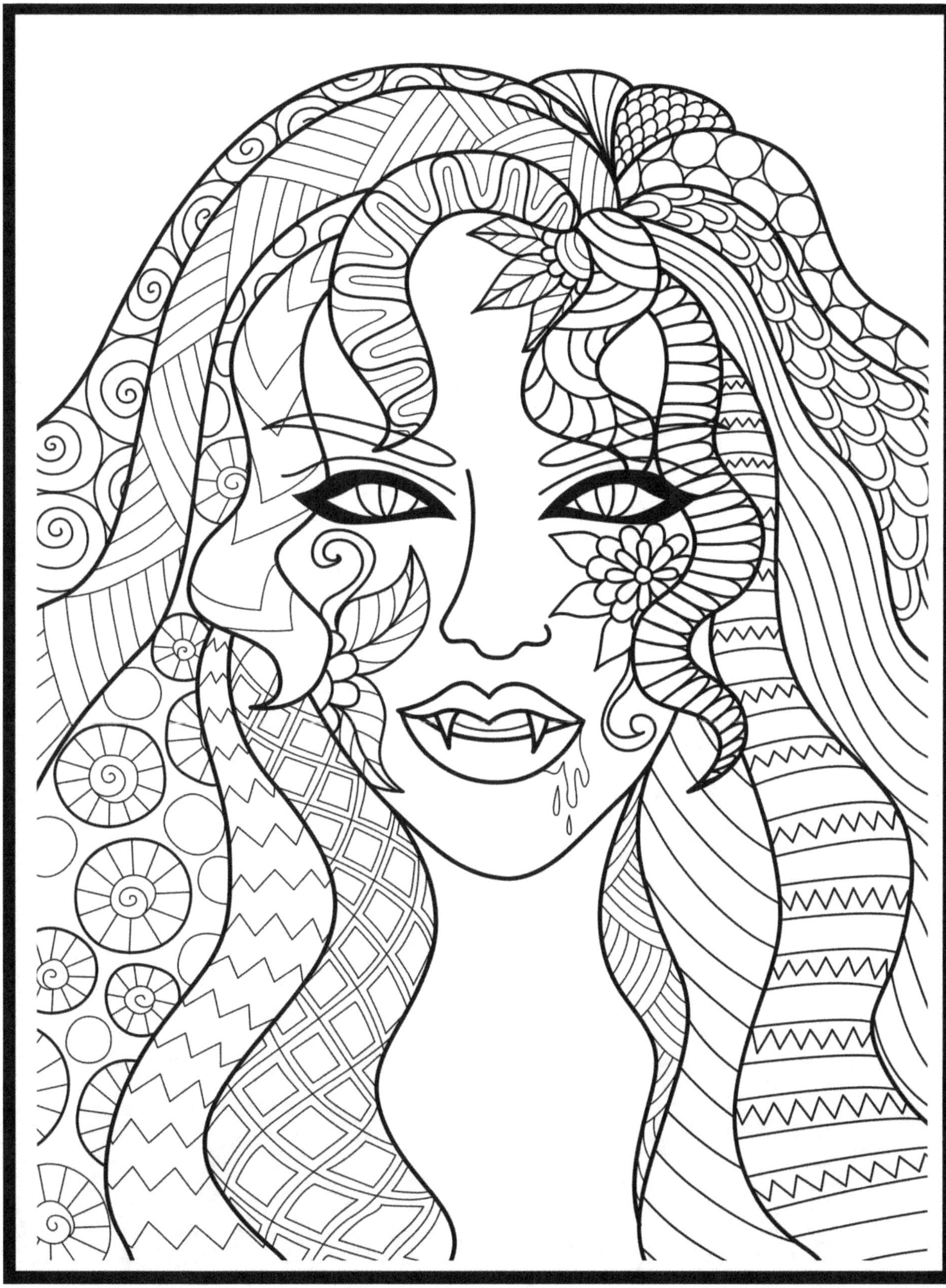

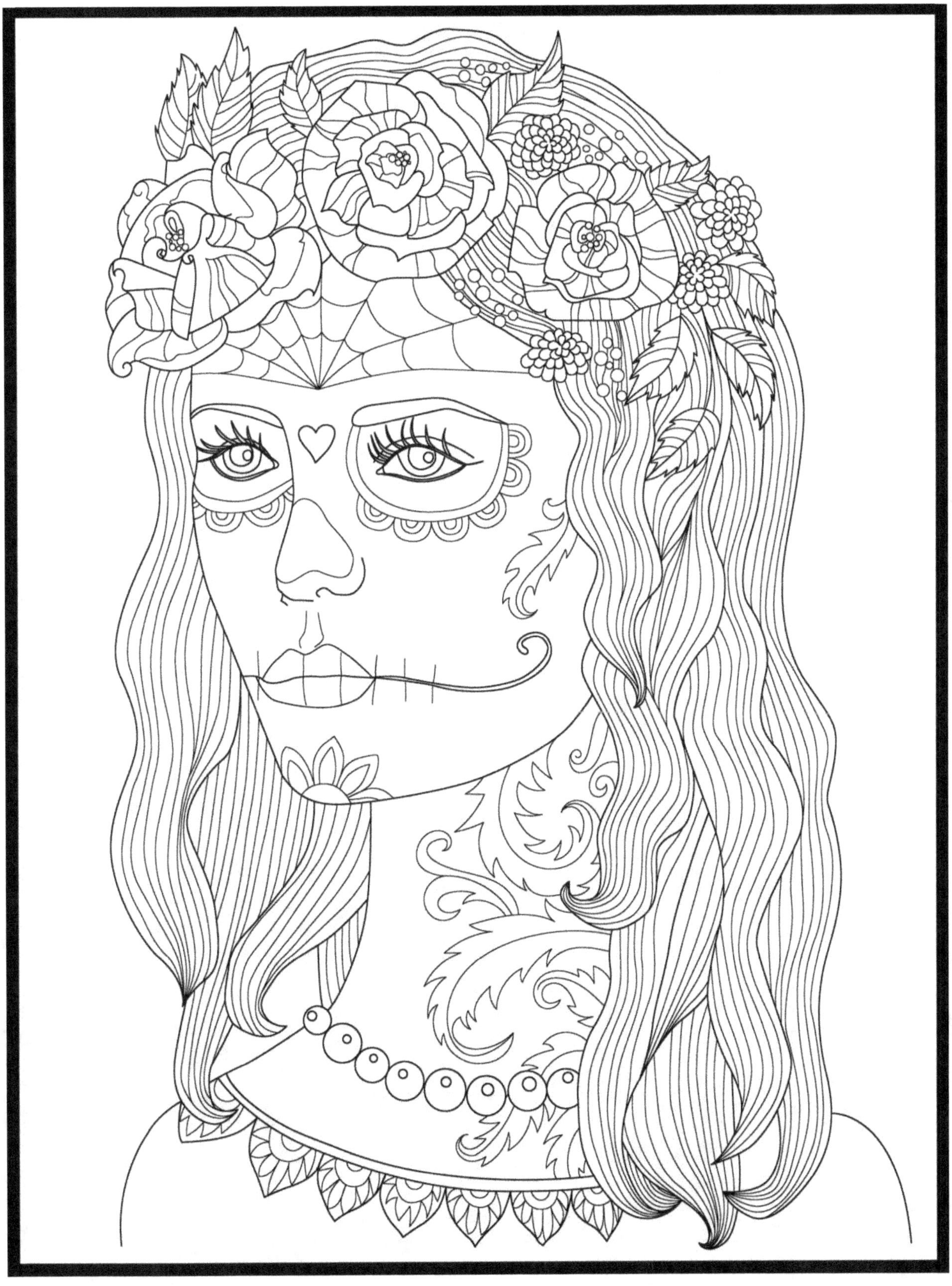

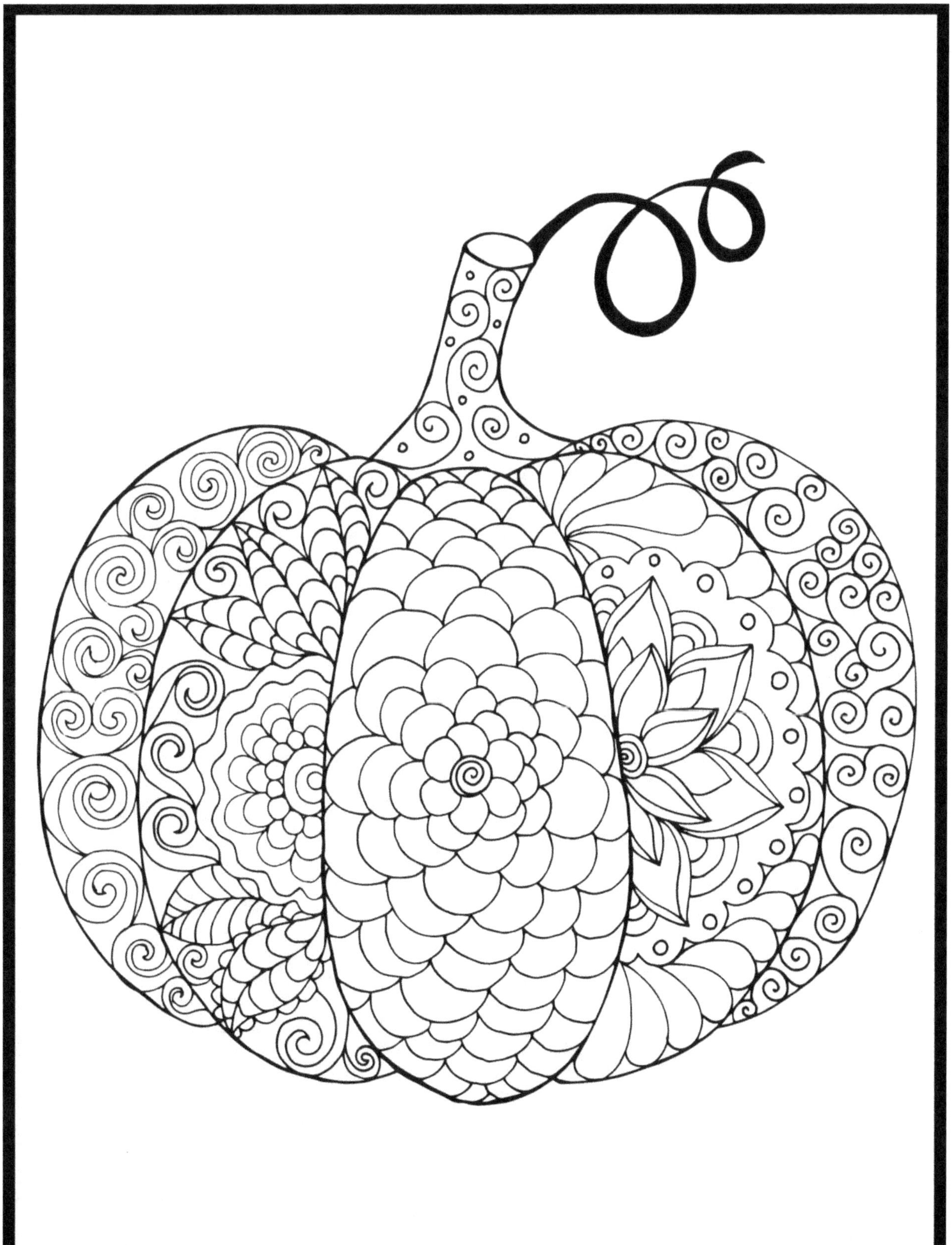

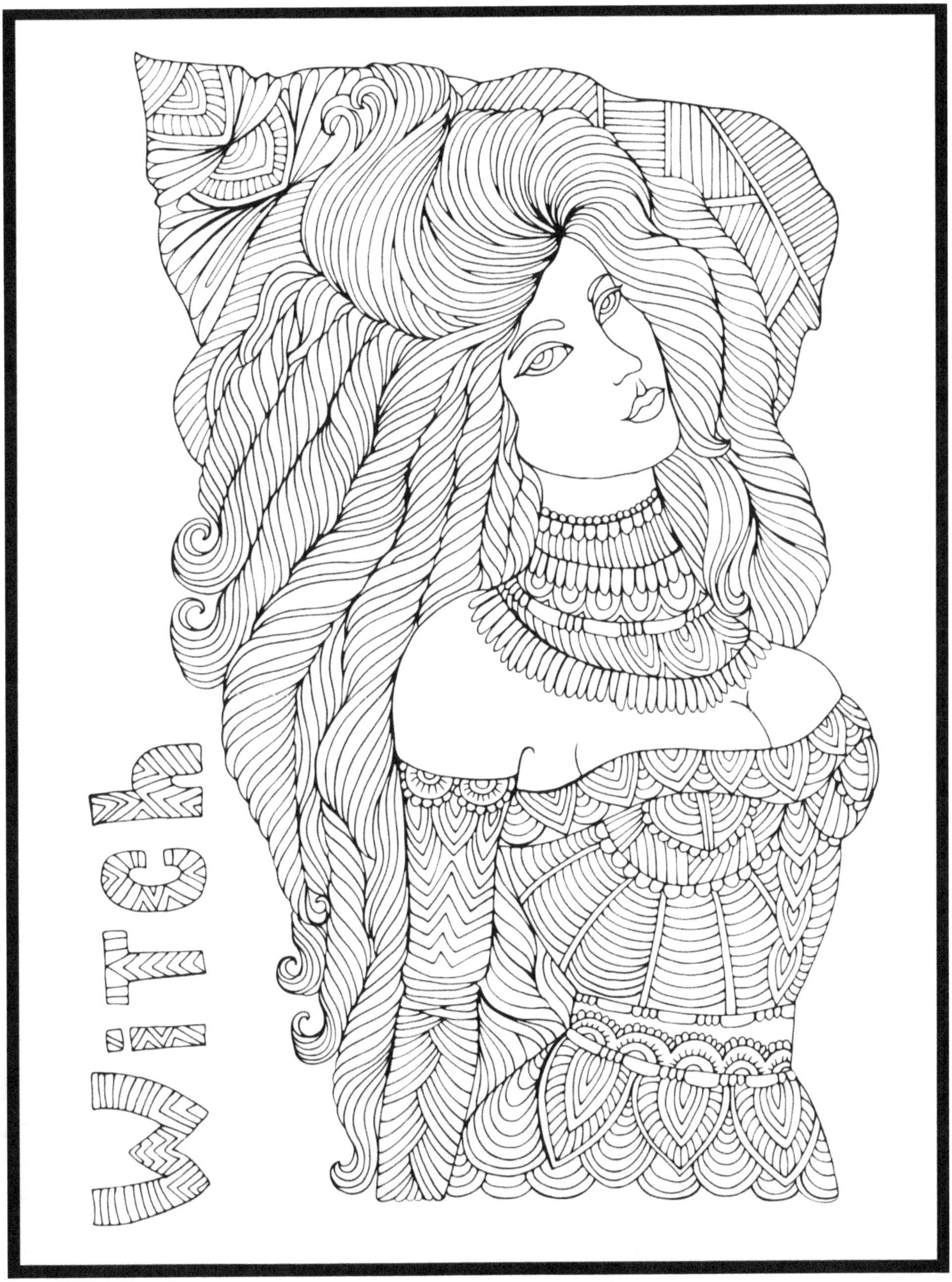
Witch

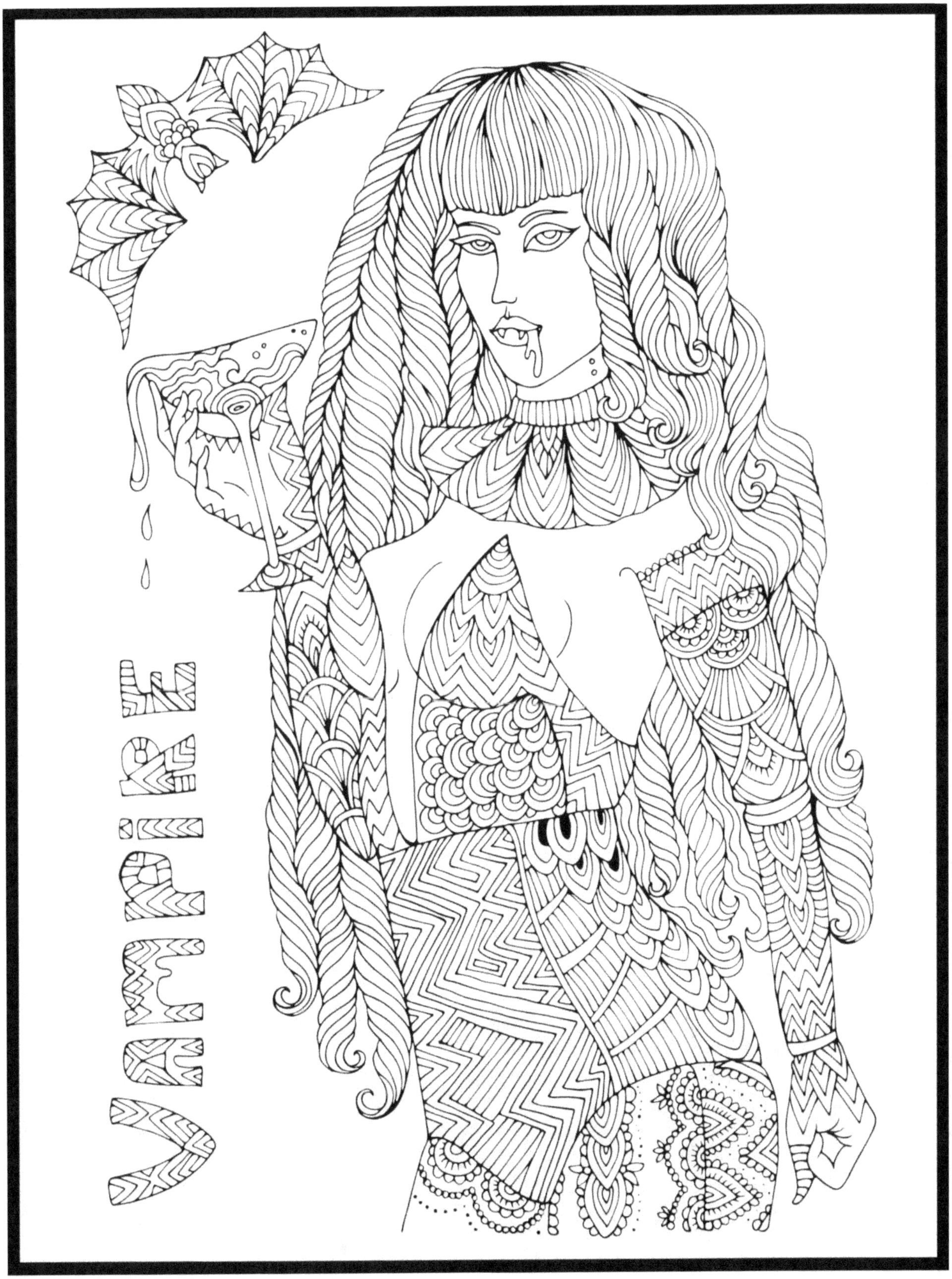
VAMPIRE

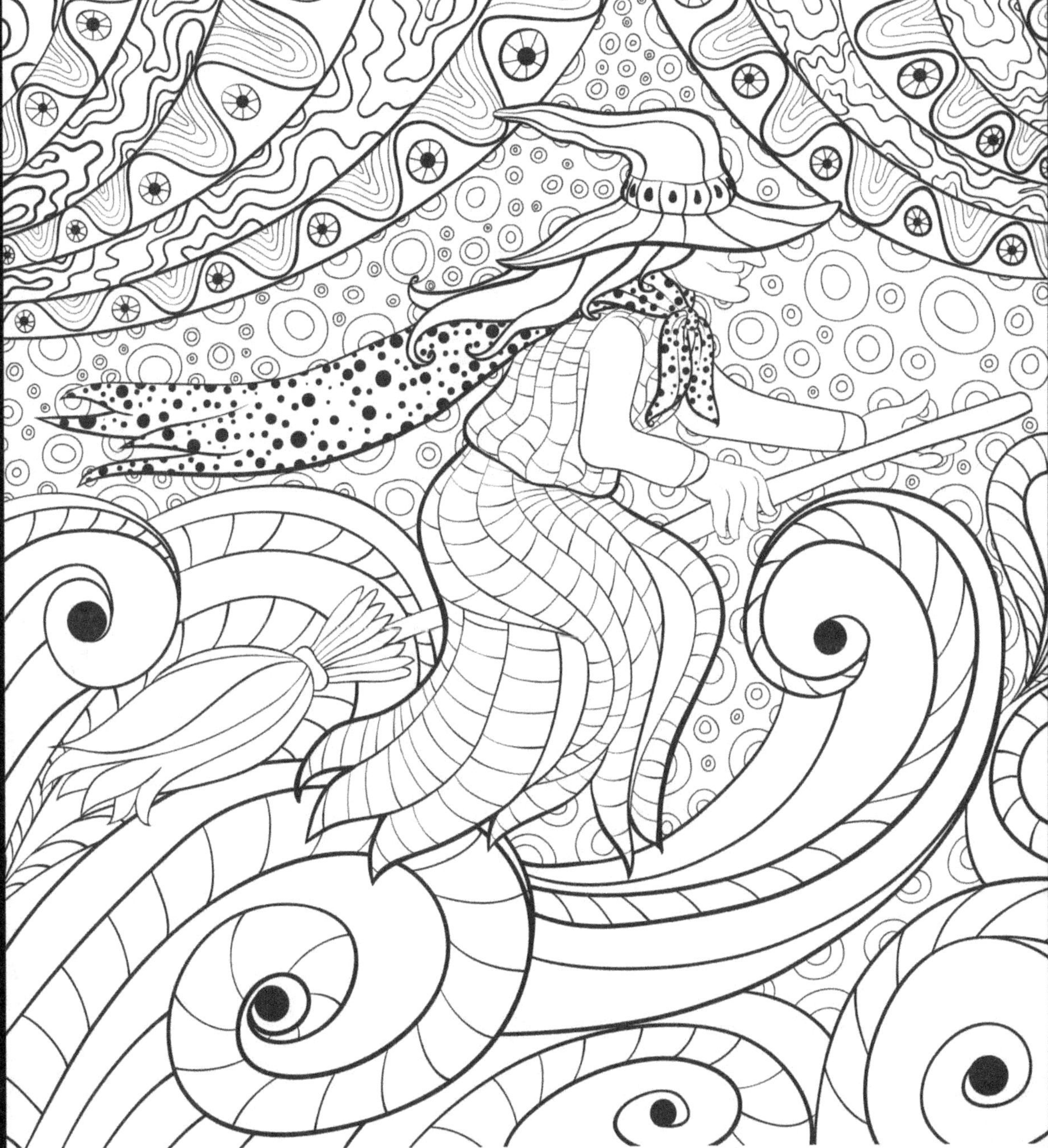

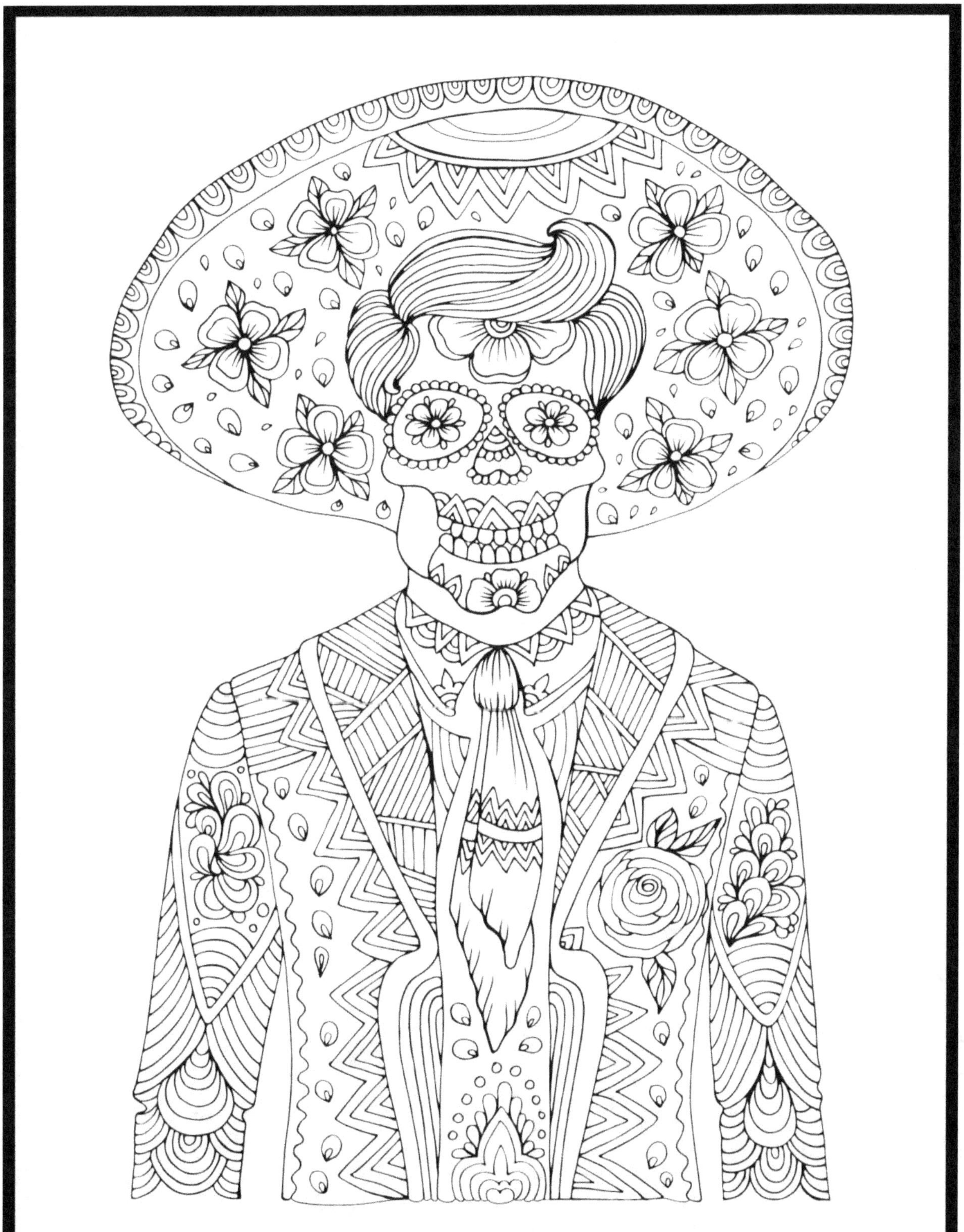

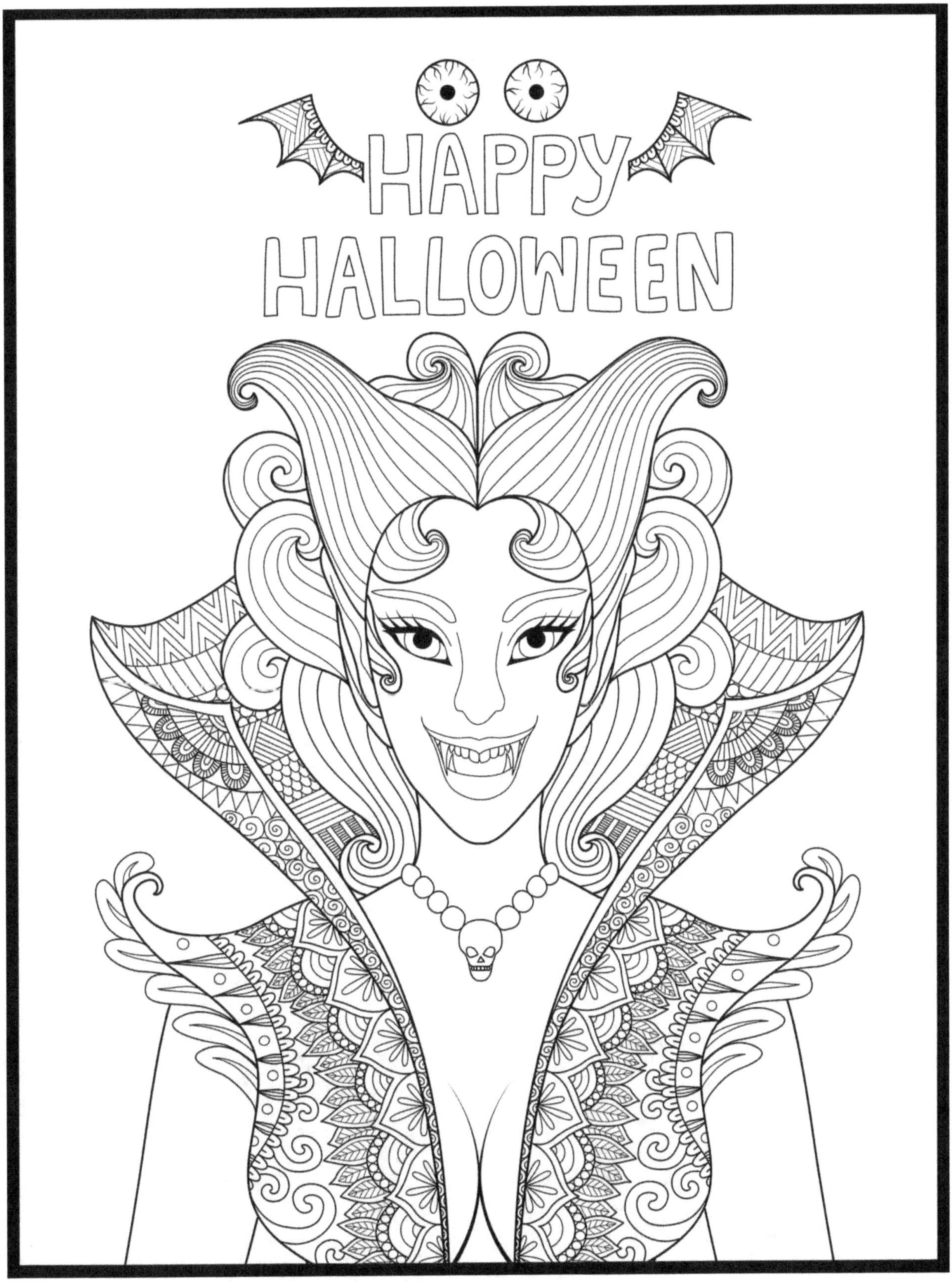
HAPPY
HALLOWEEN

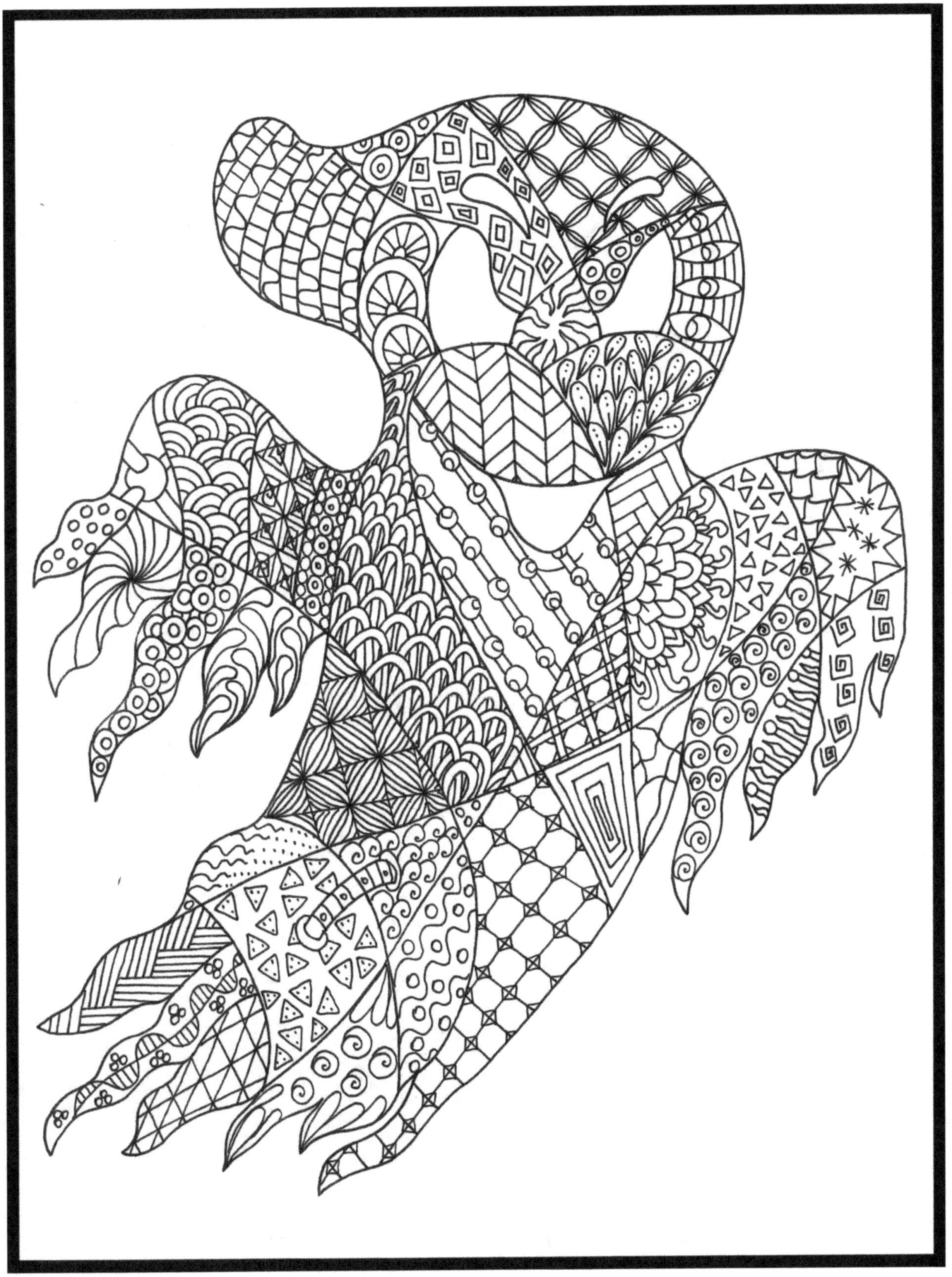

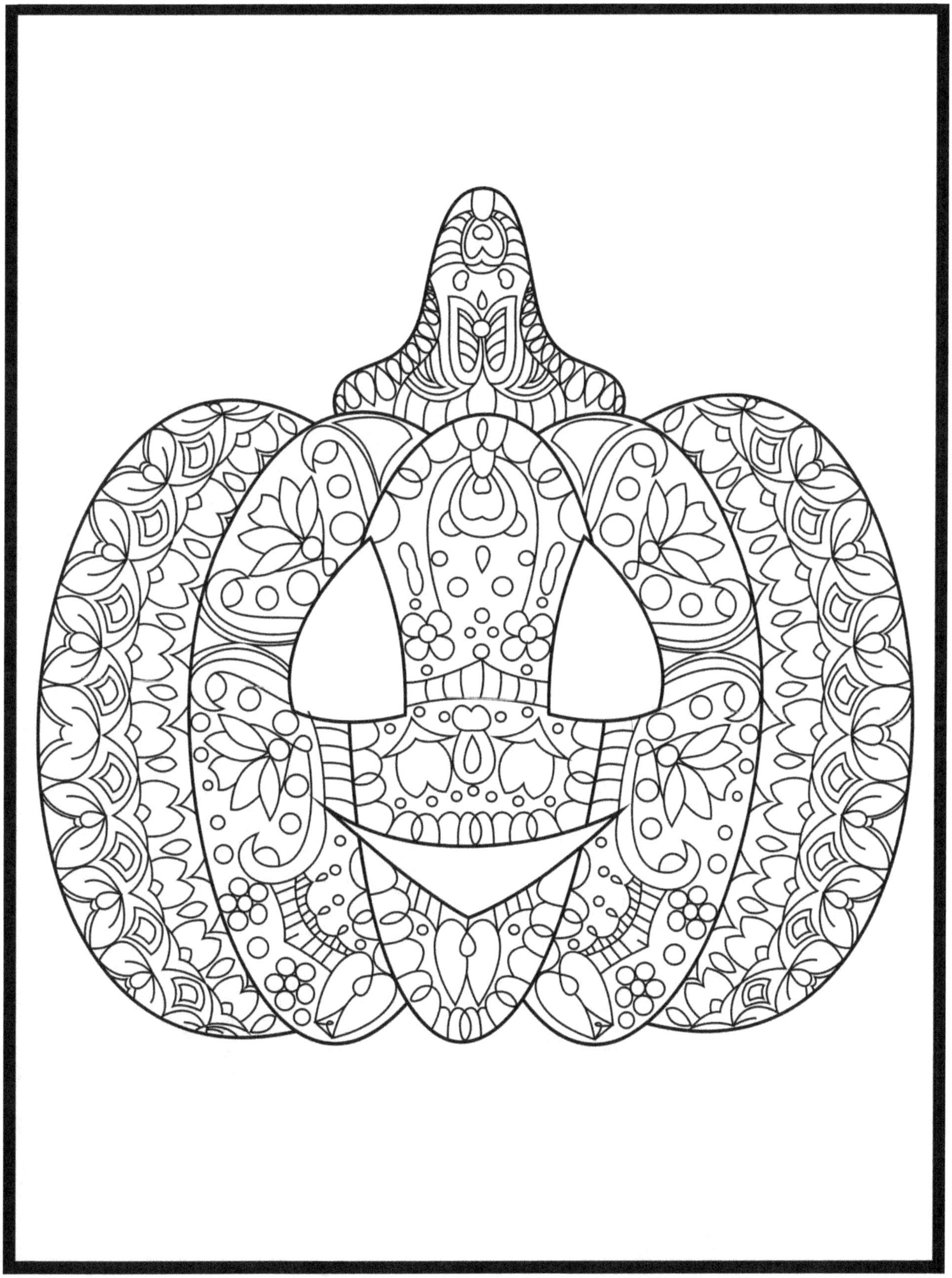

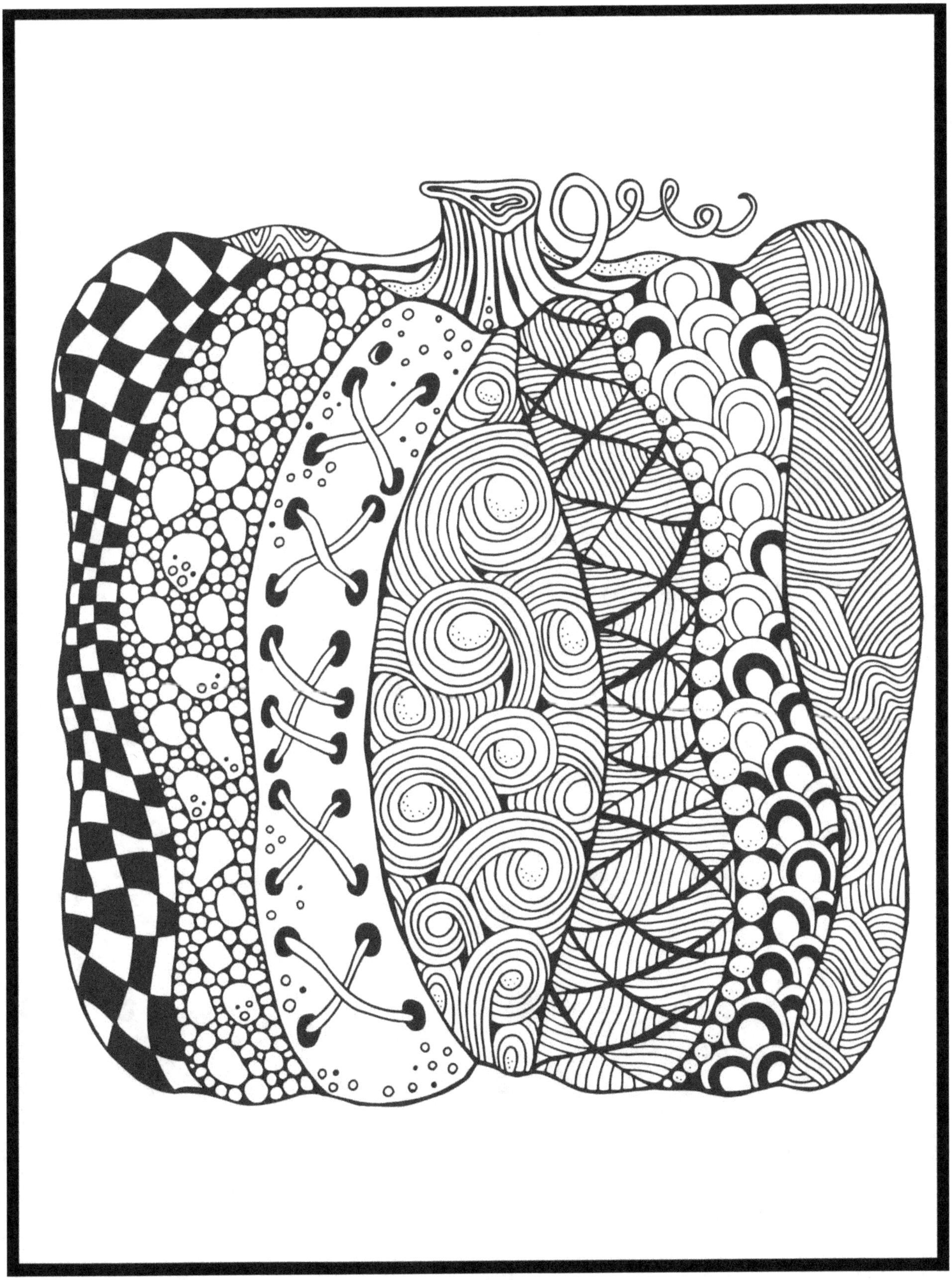

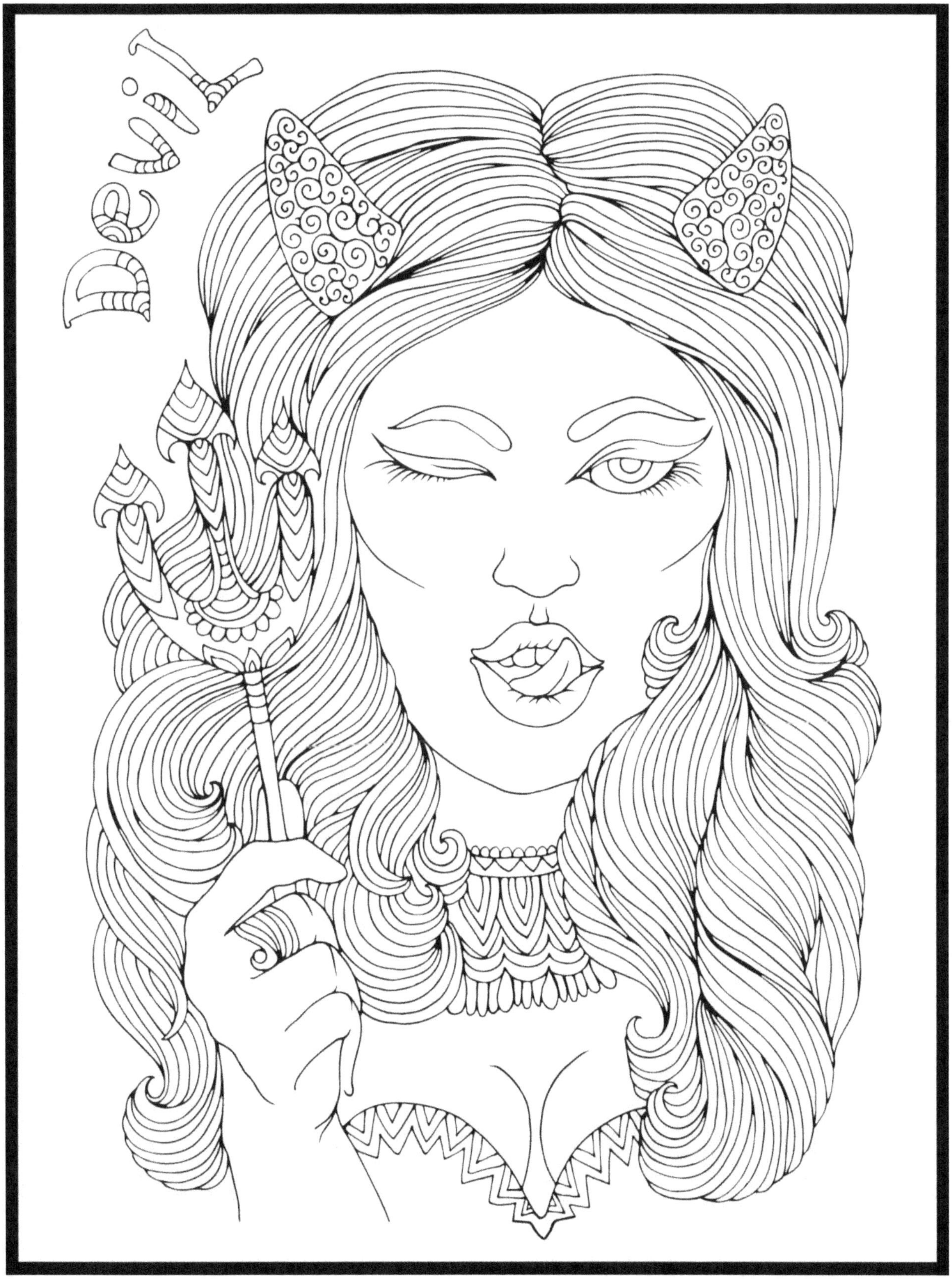
Devil

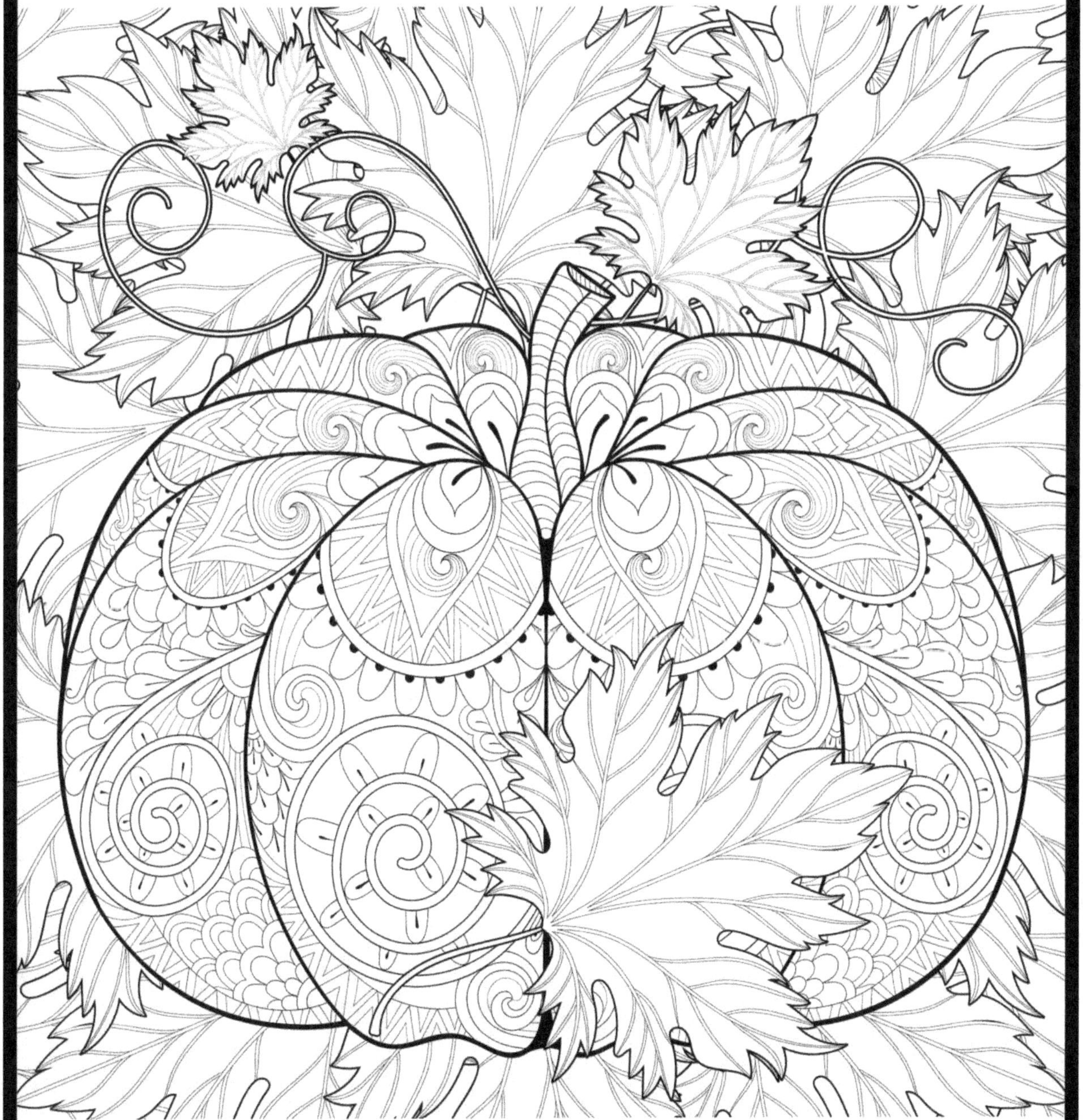

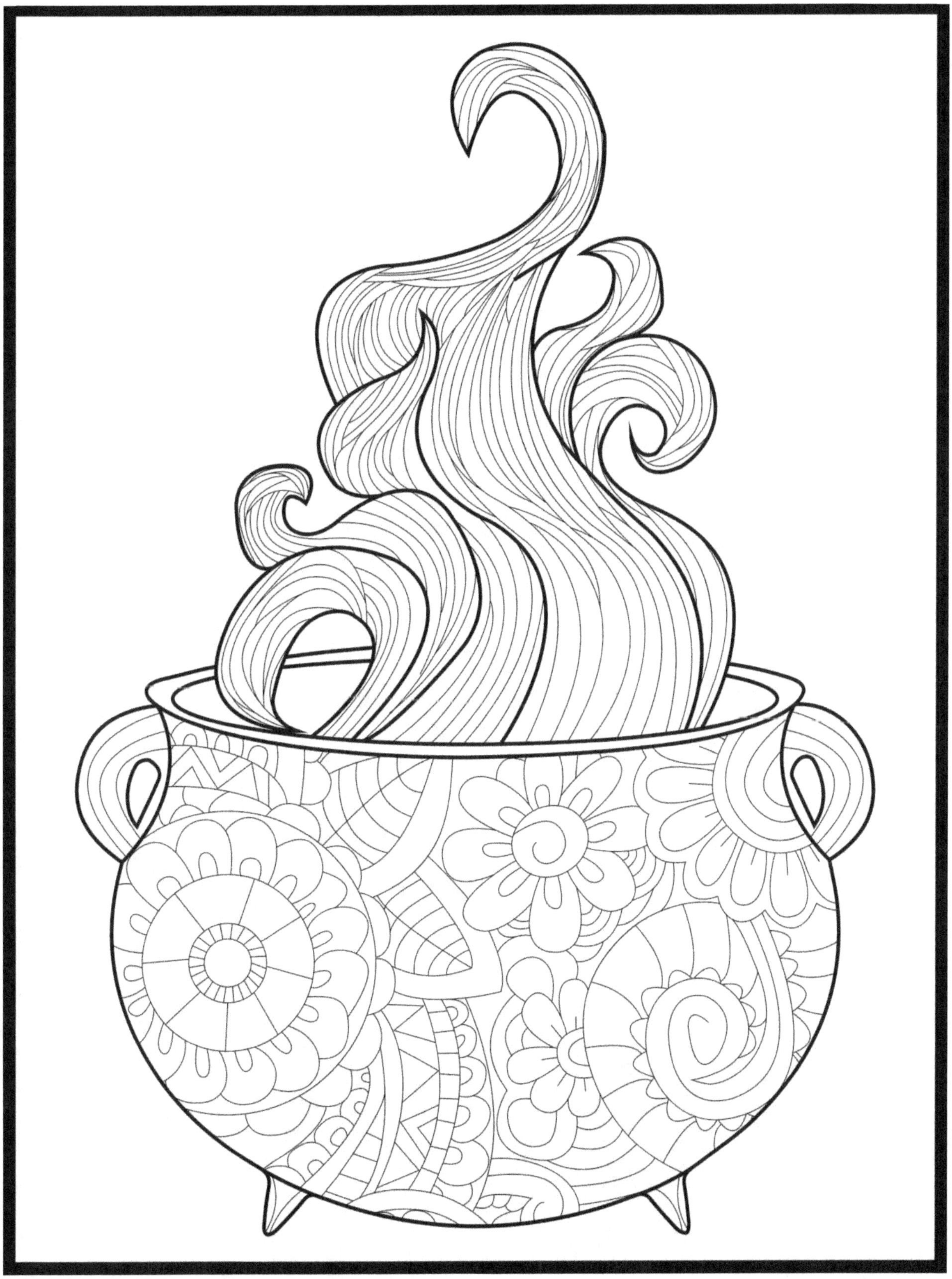

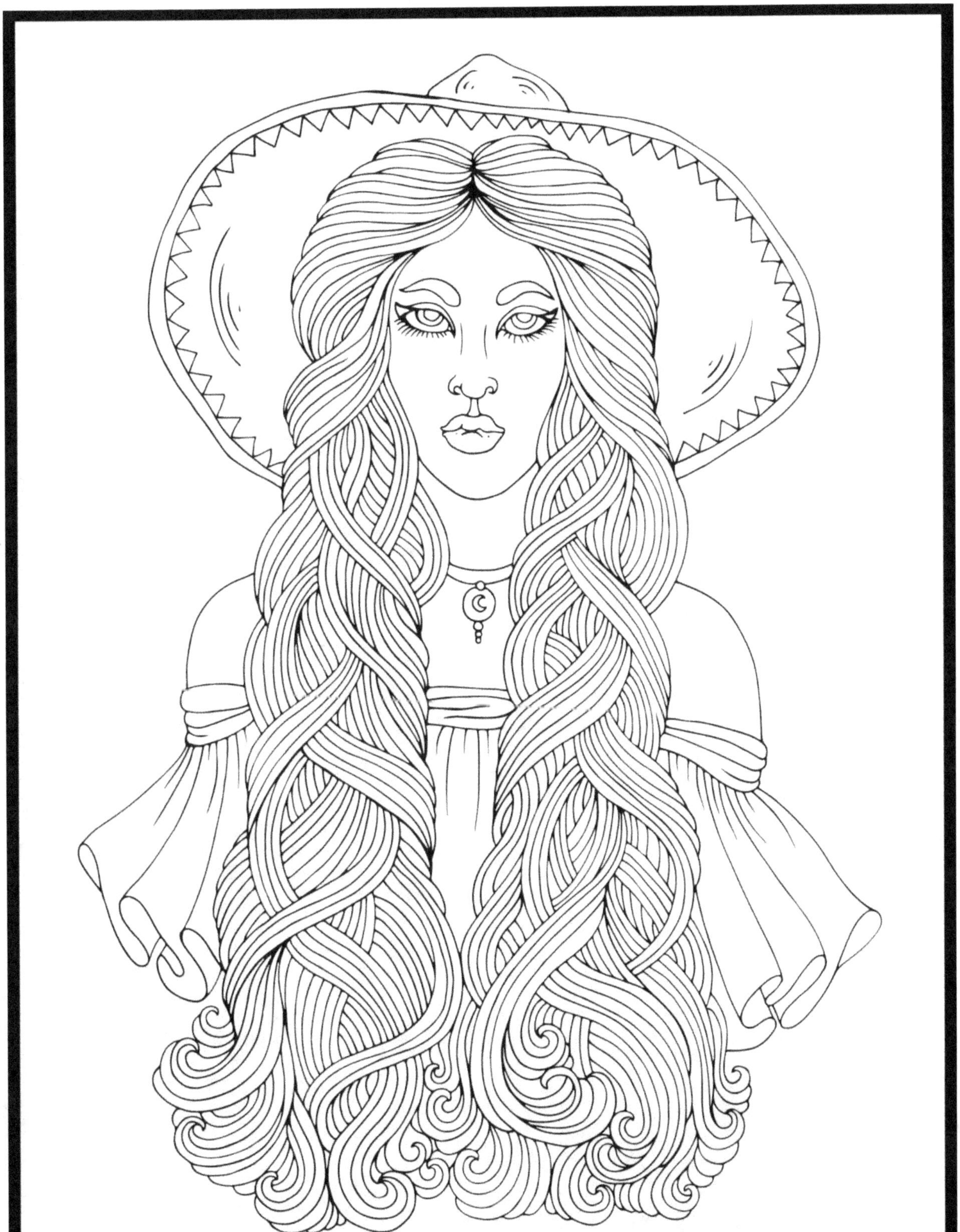

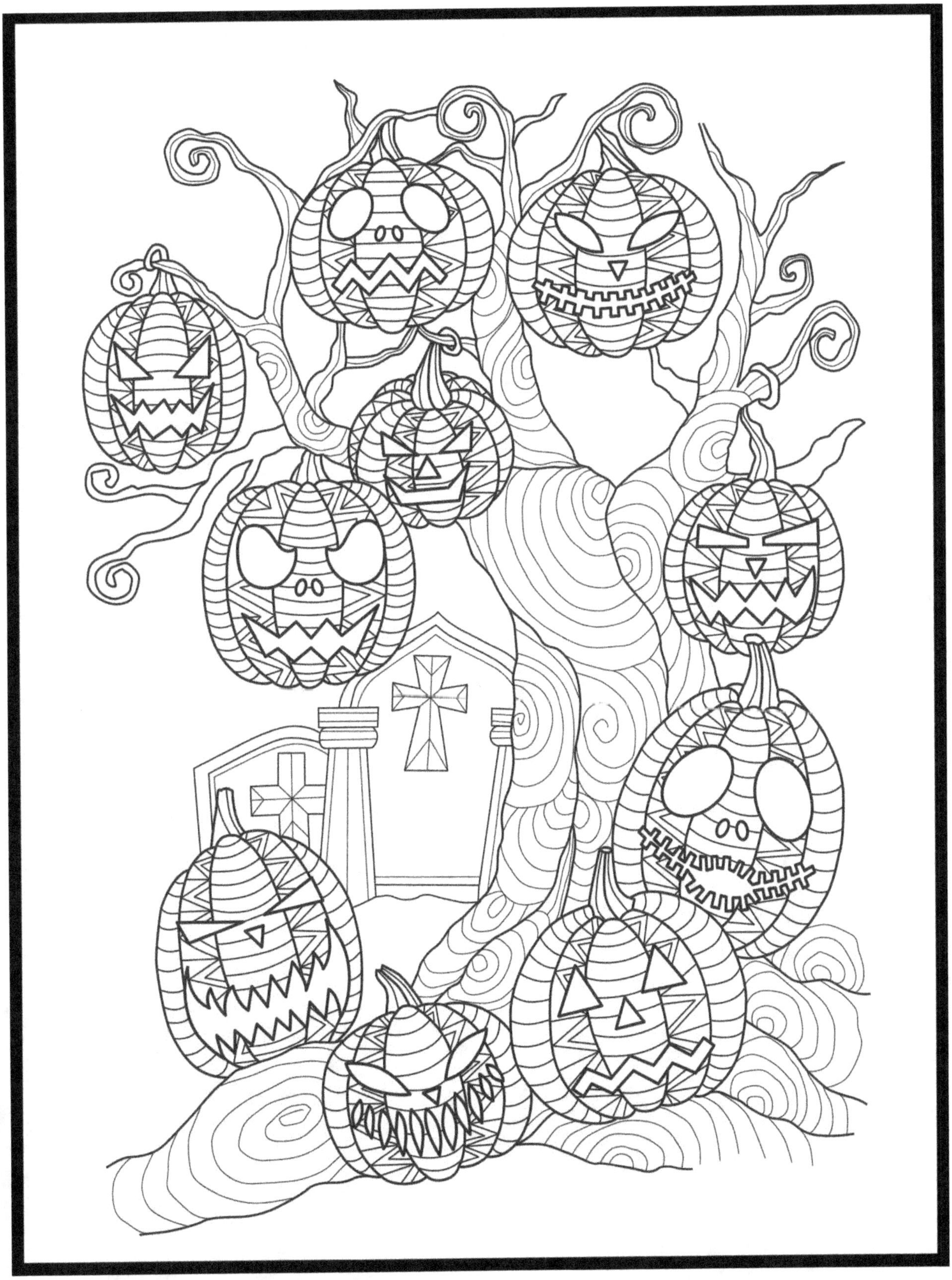

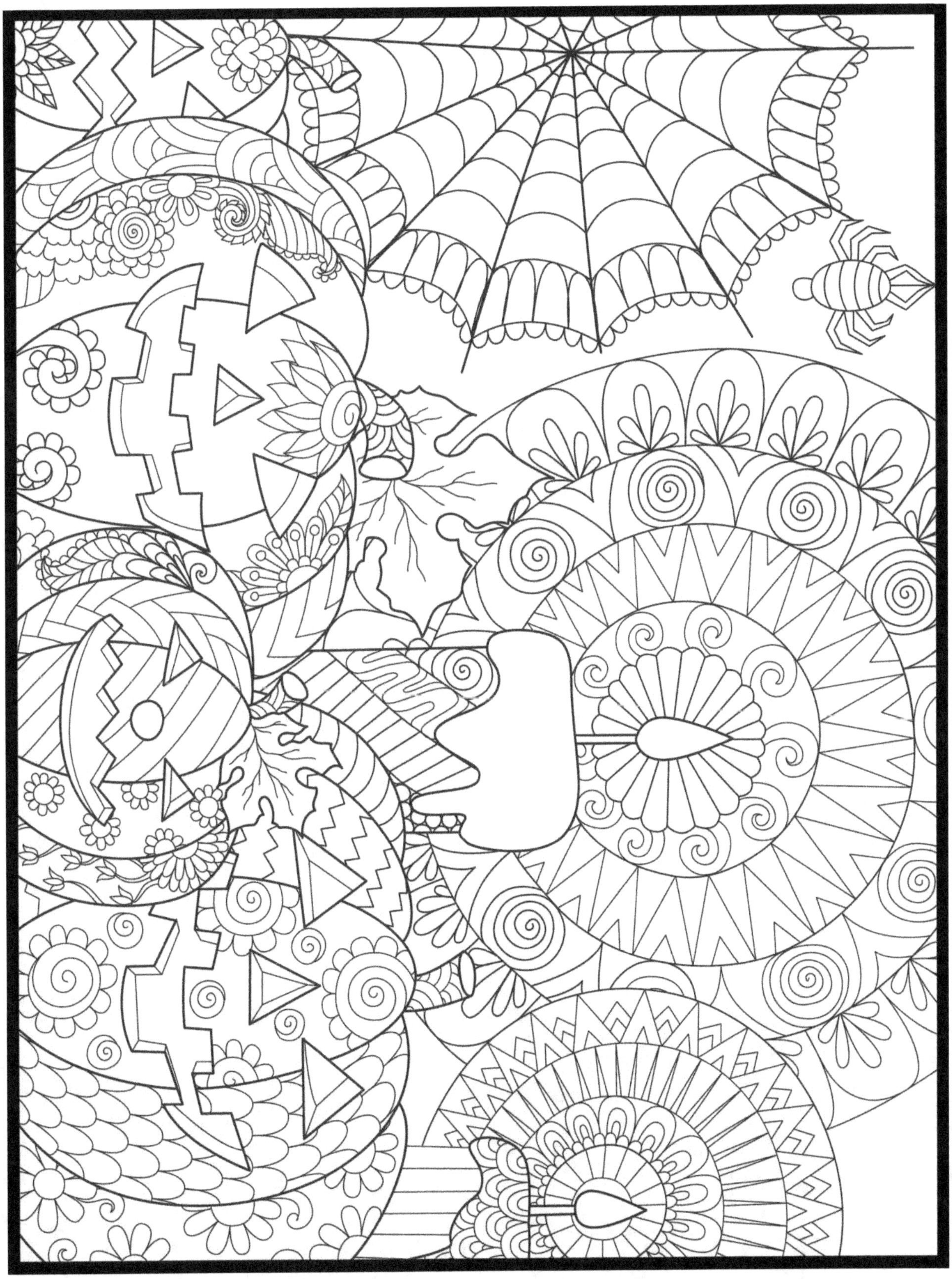

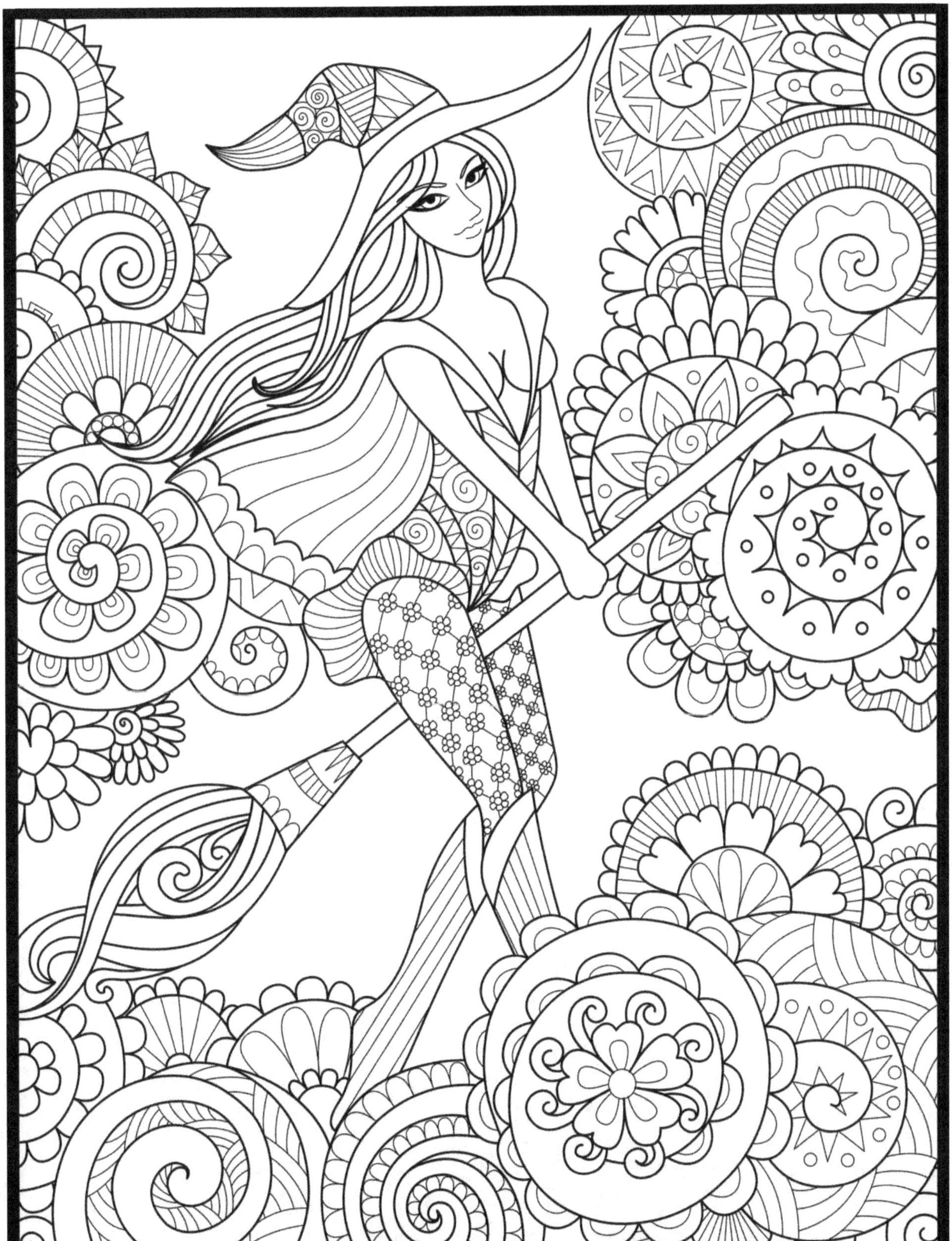

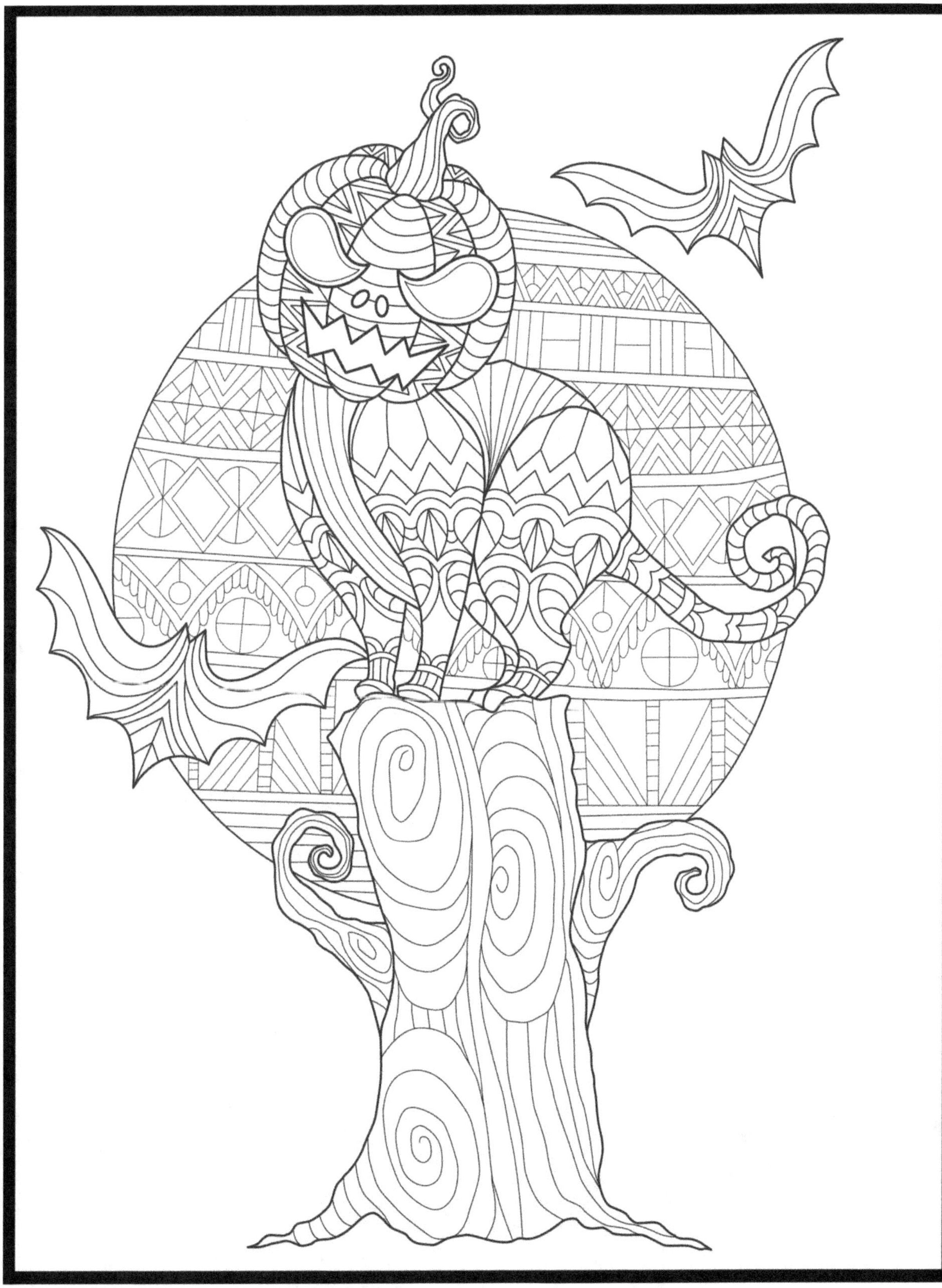

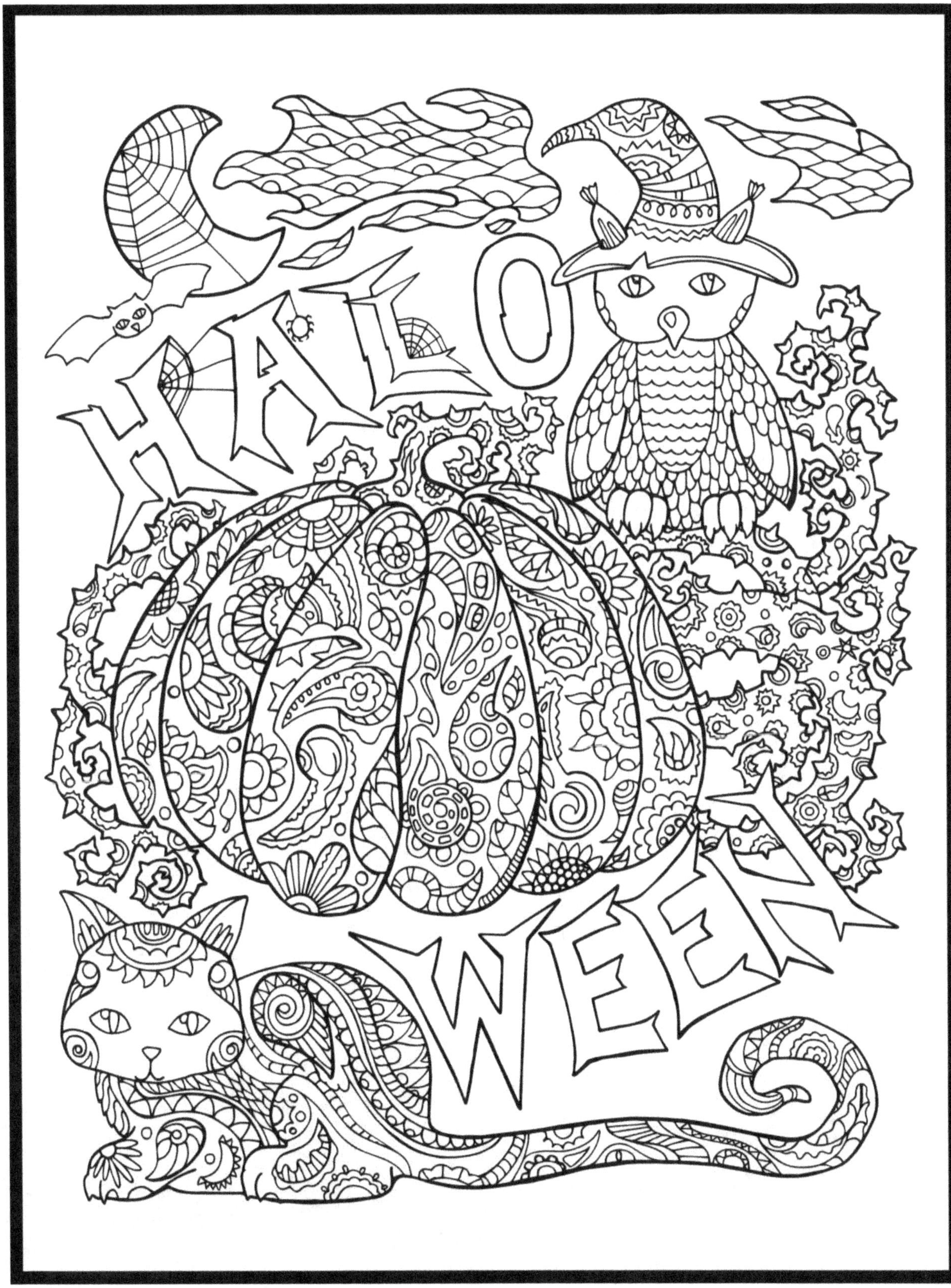
HALO
WEEN

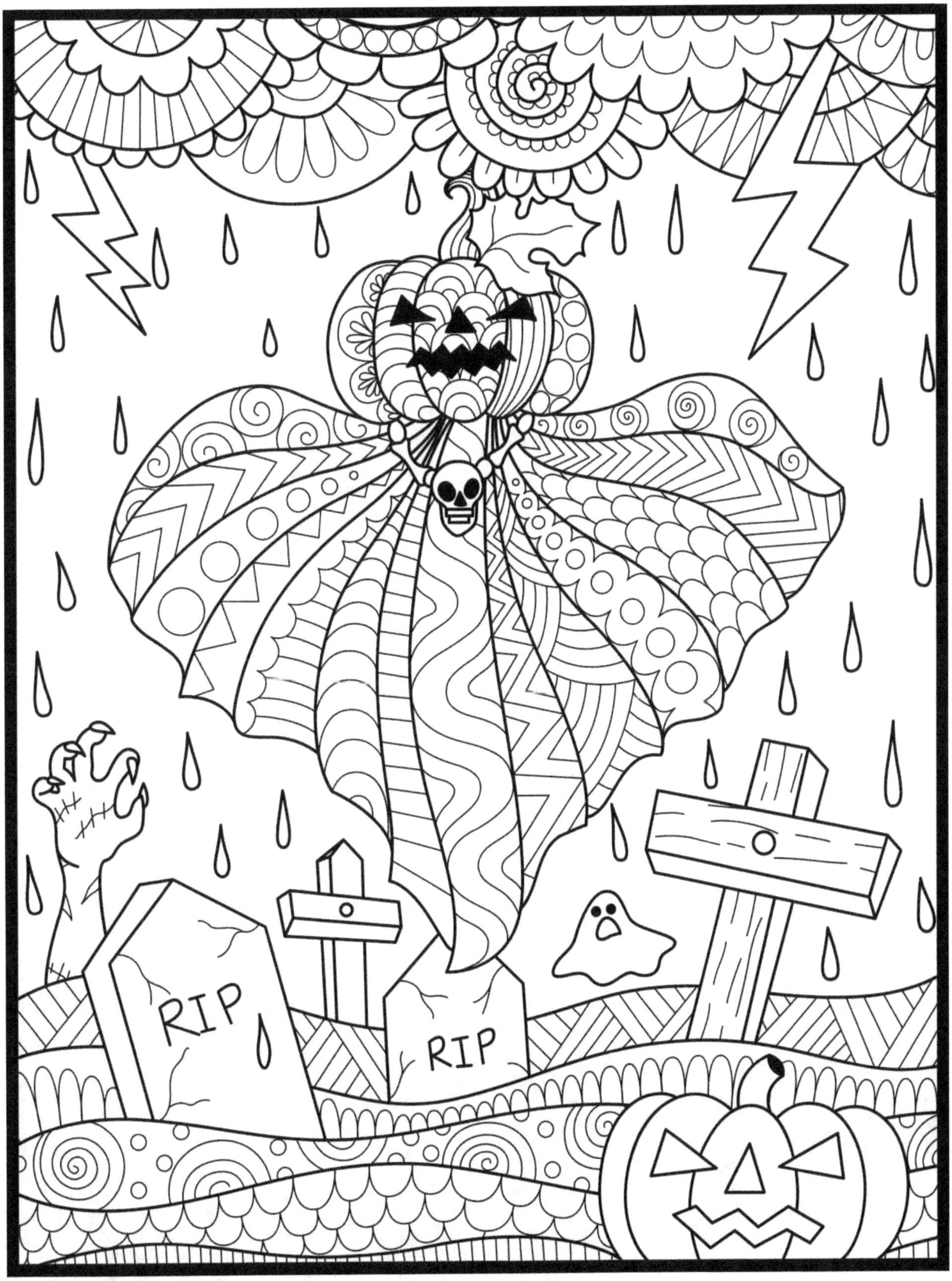

RIP
RIP

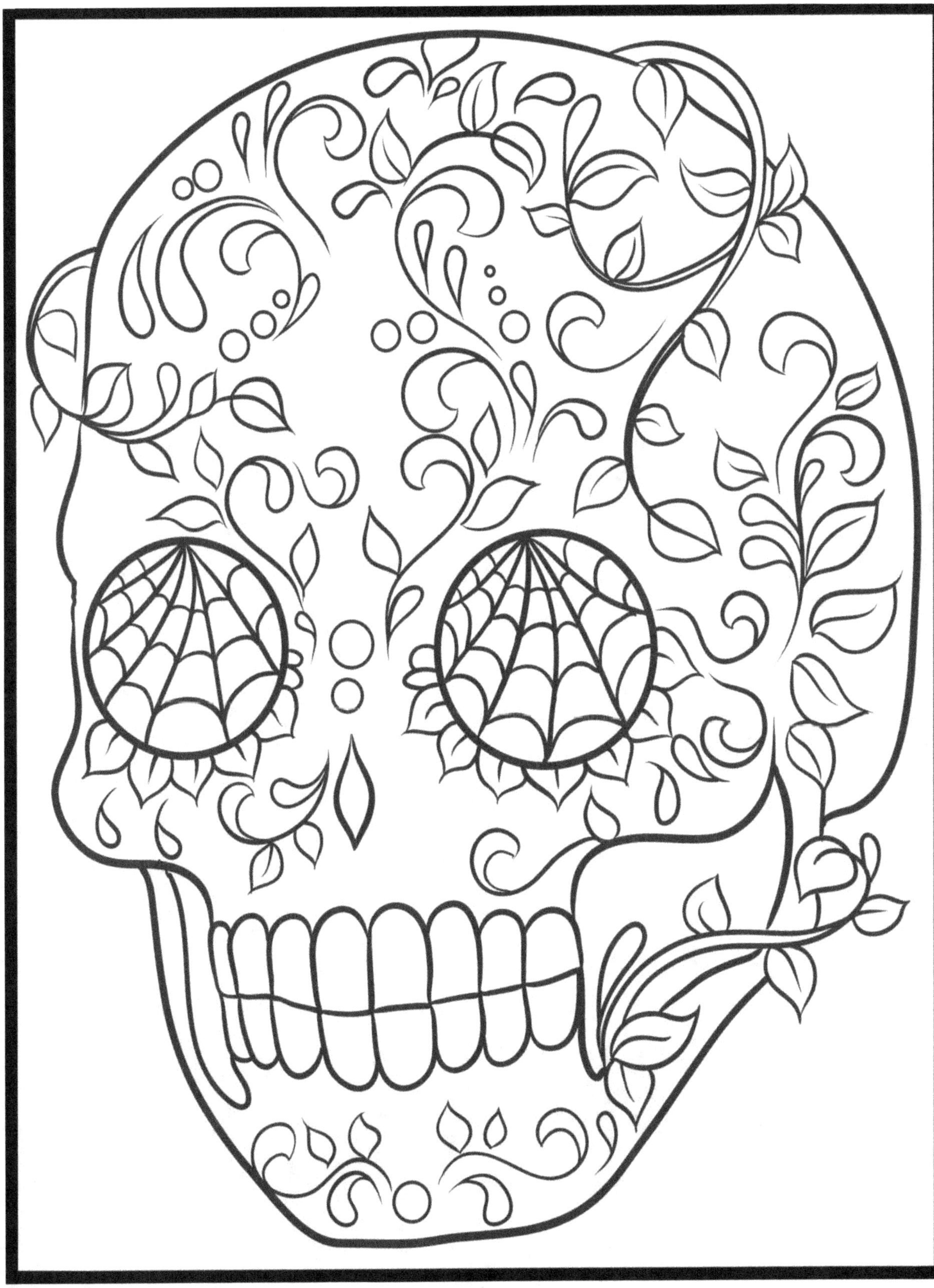

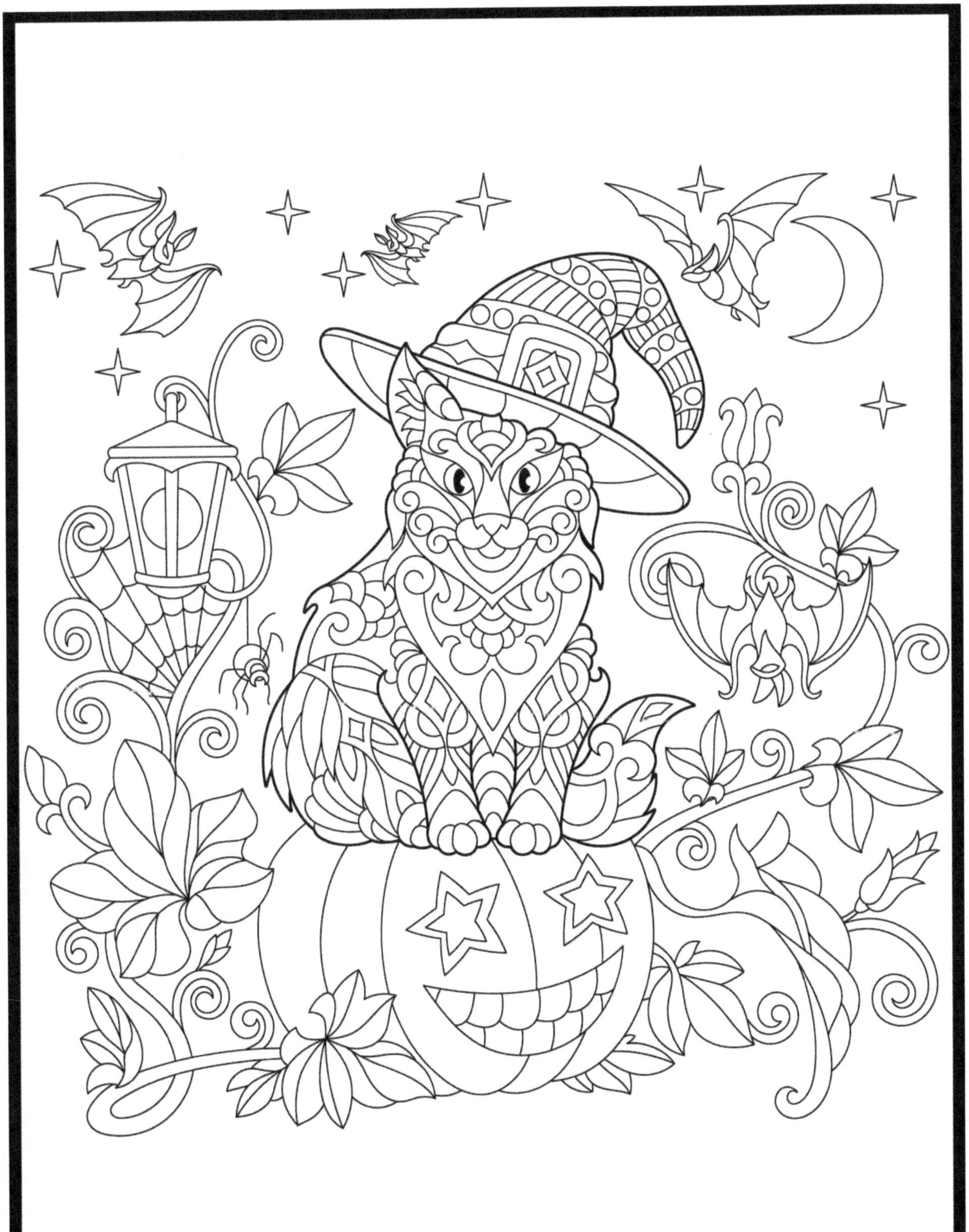

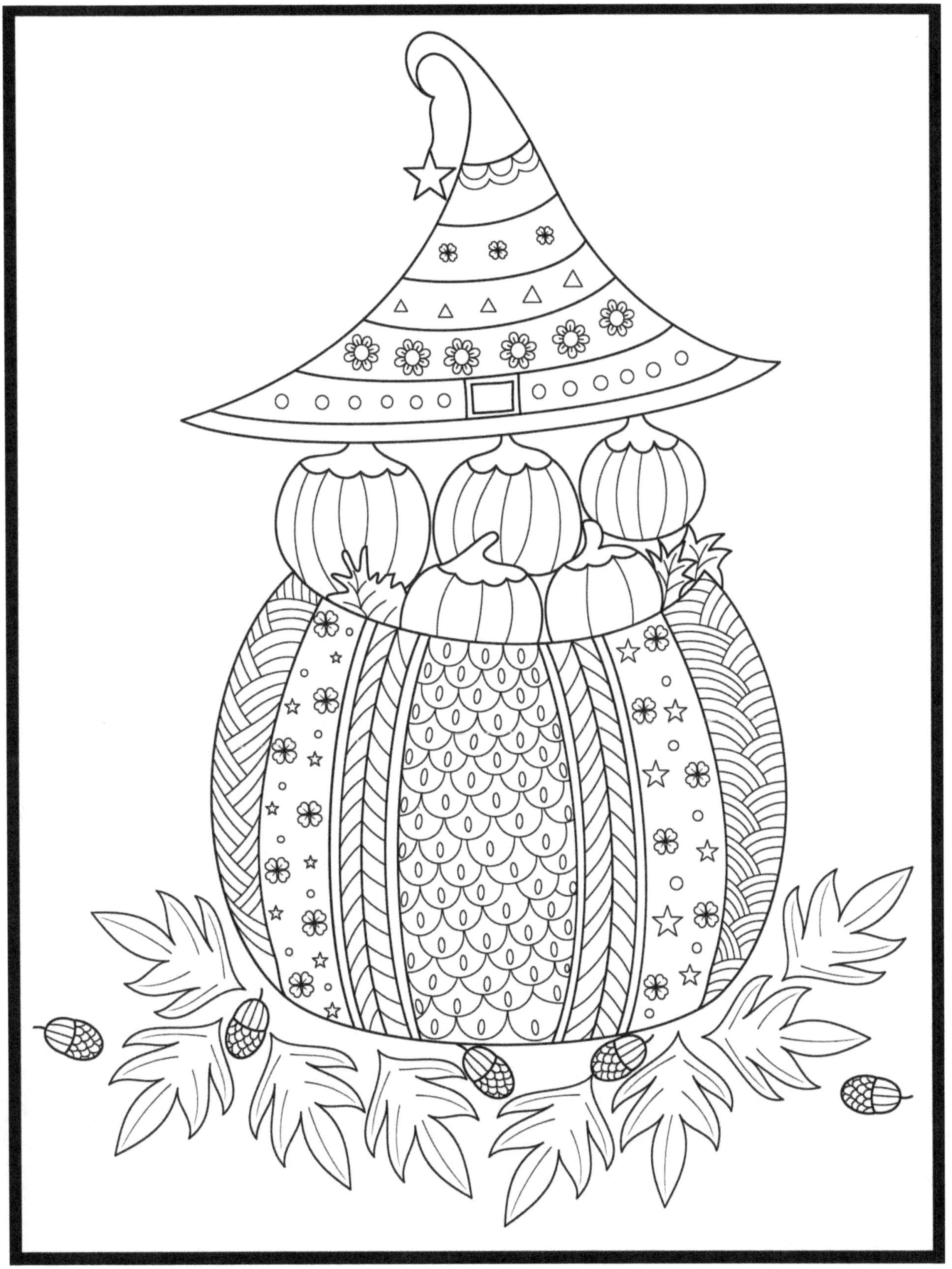

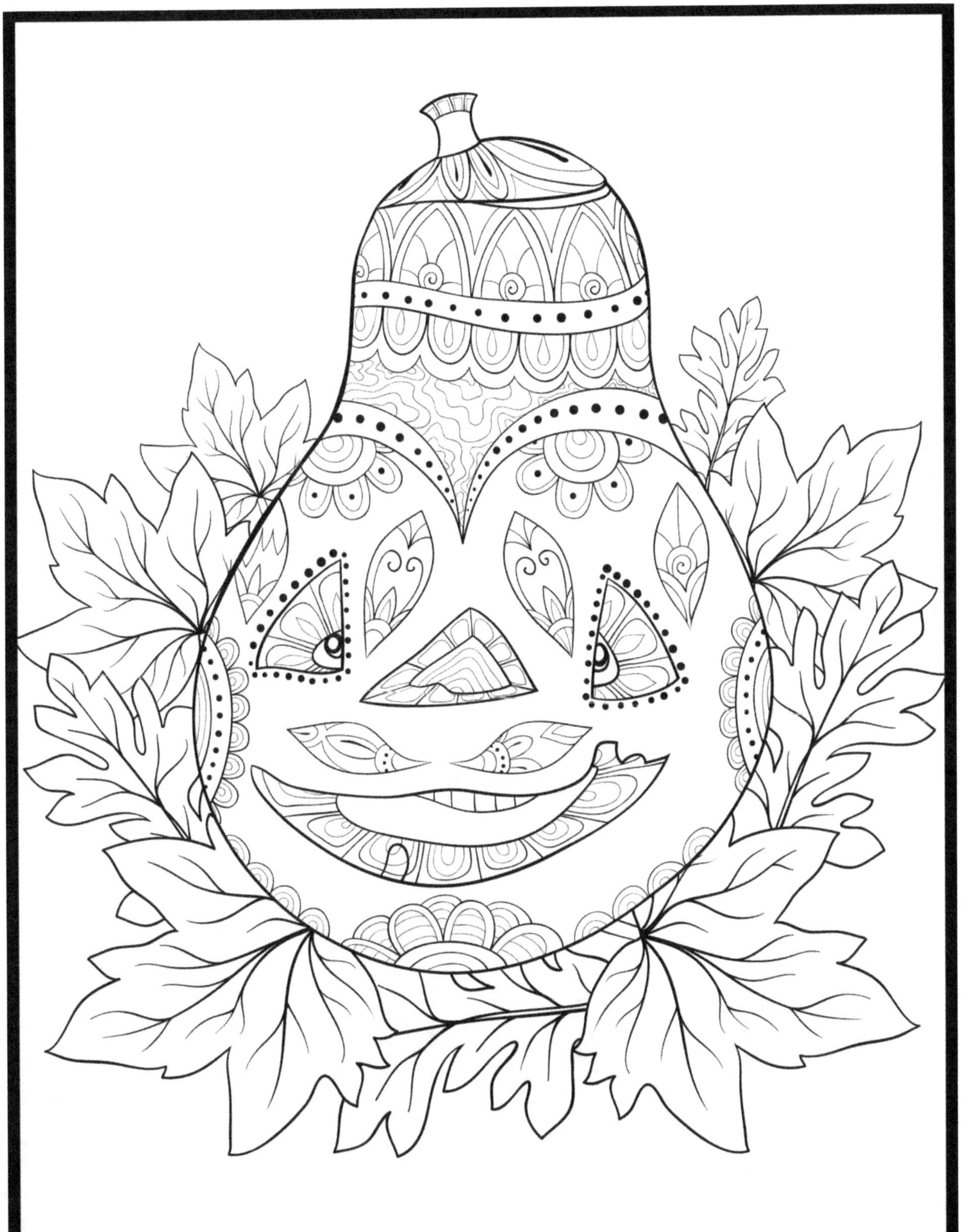

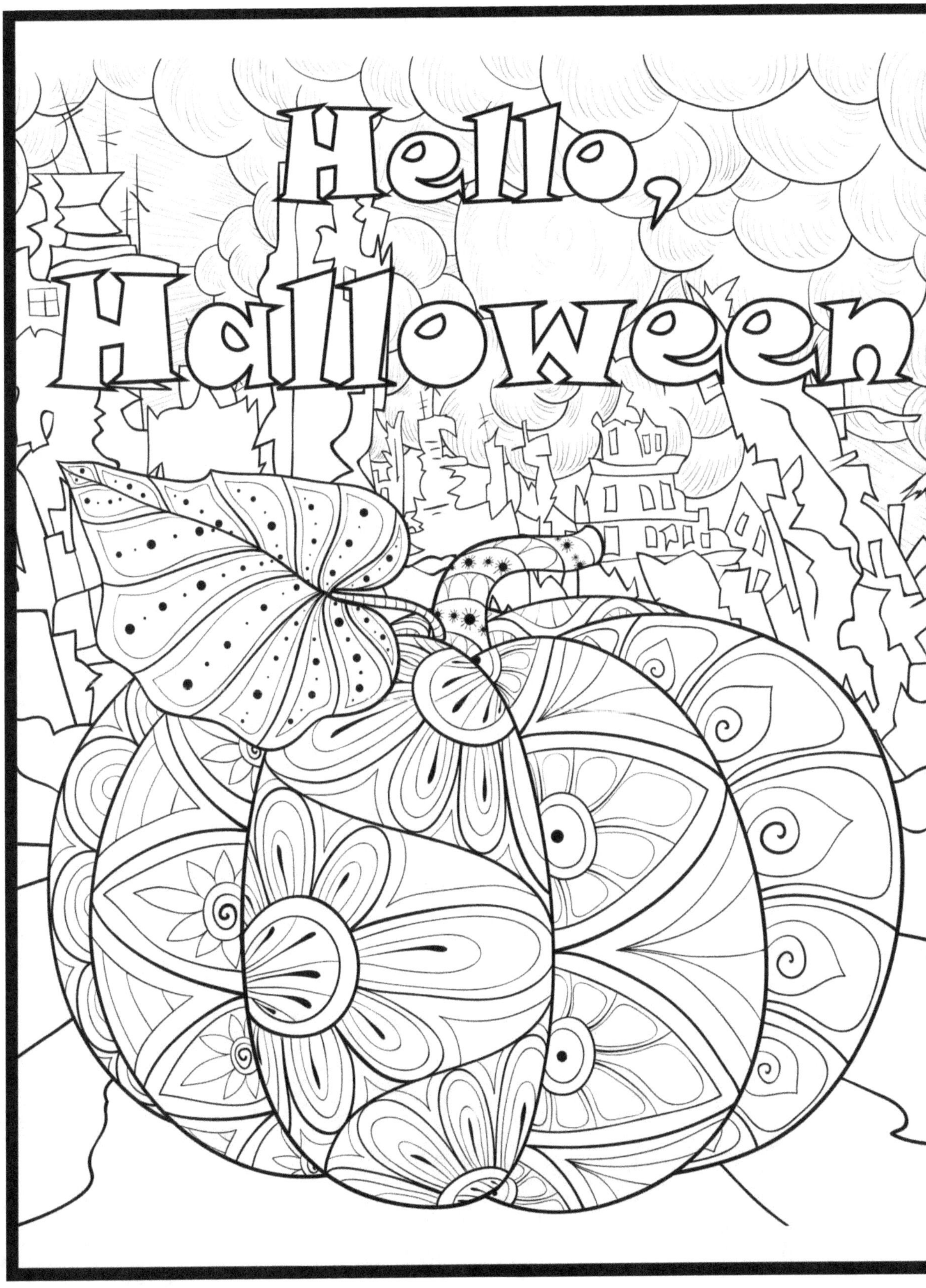
Hello,
Halloween

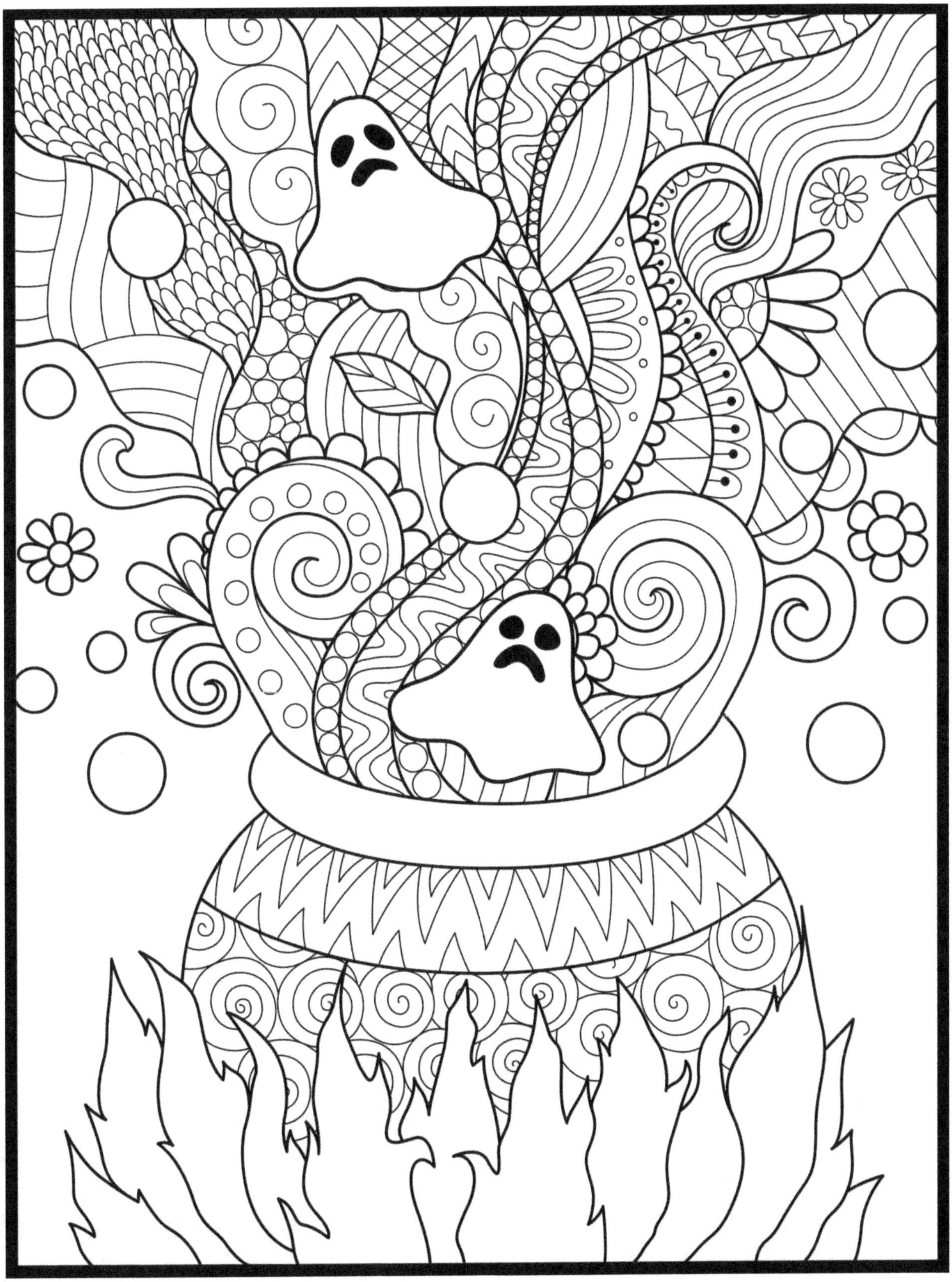

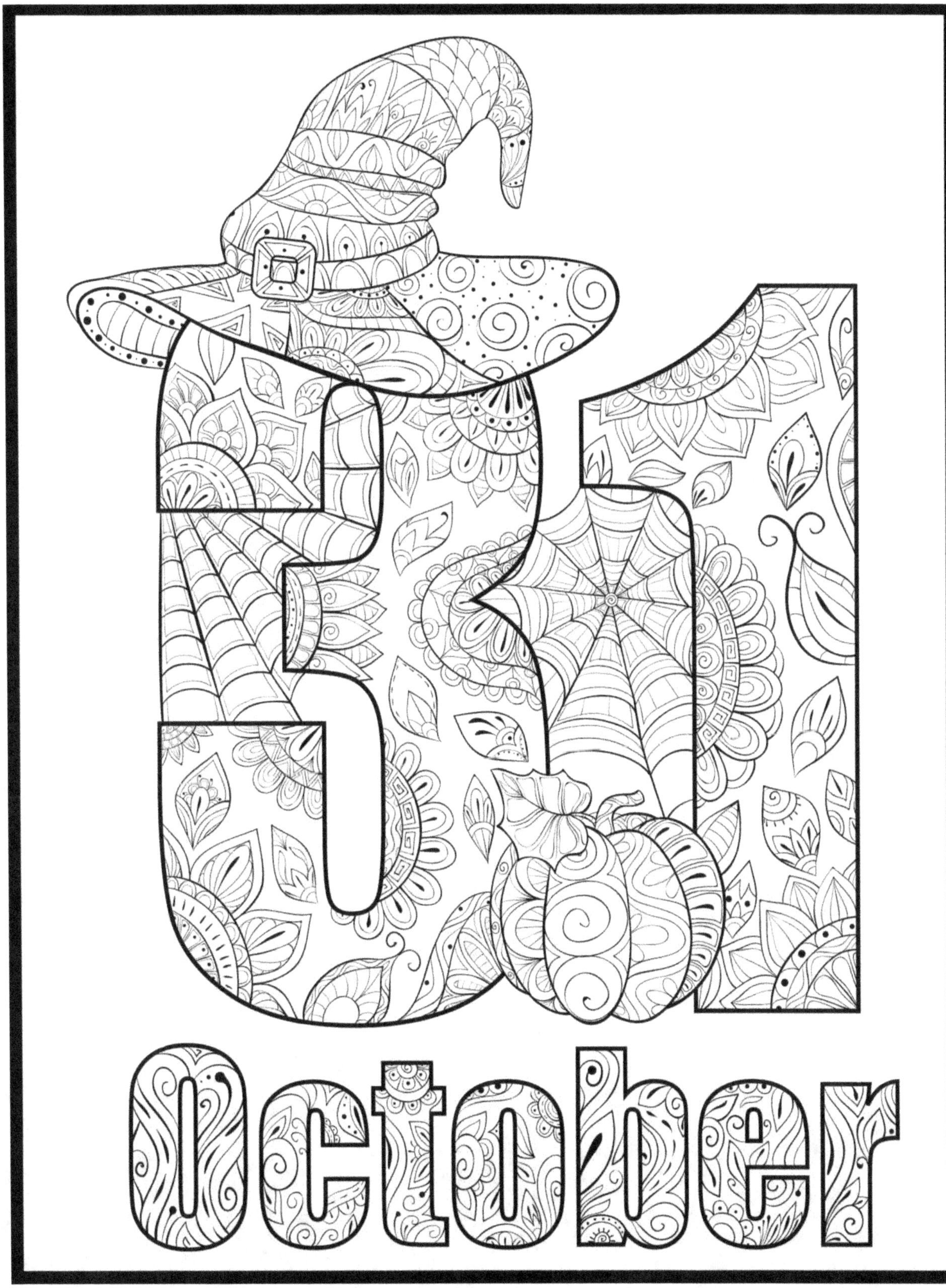
31
October

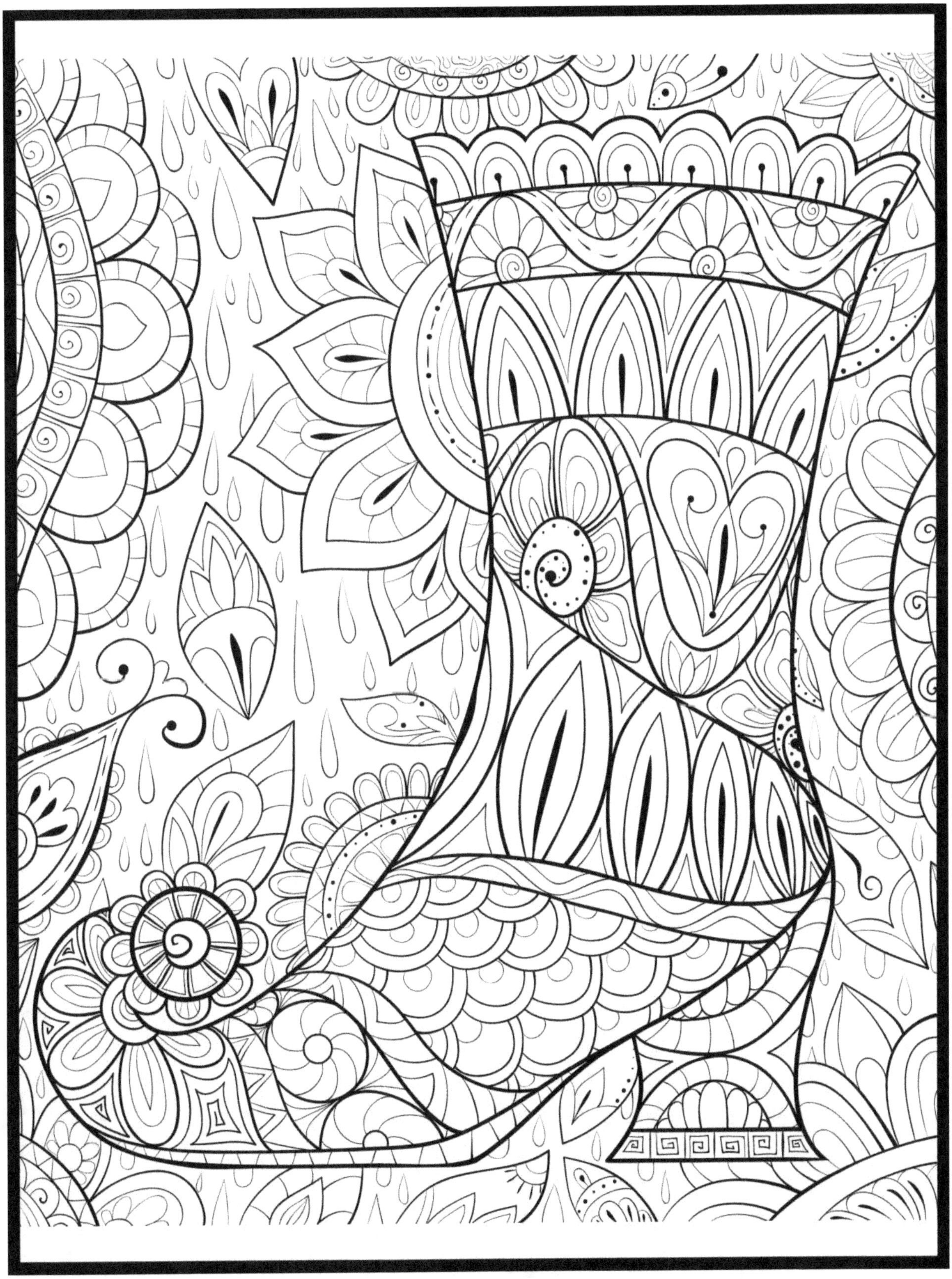

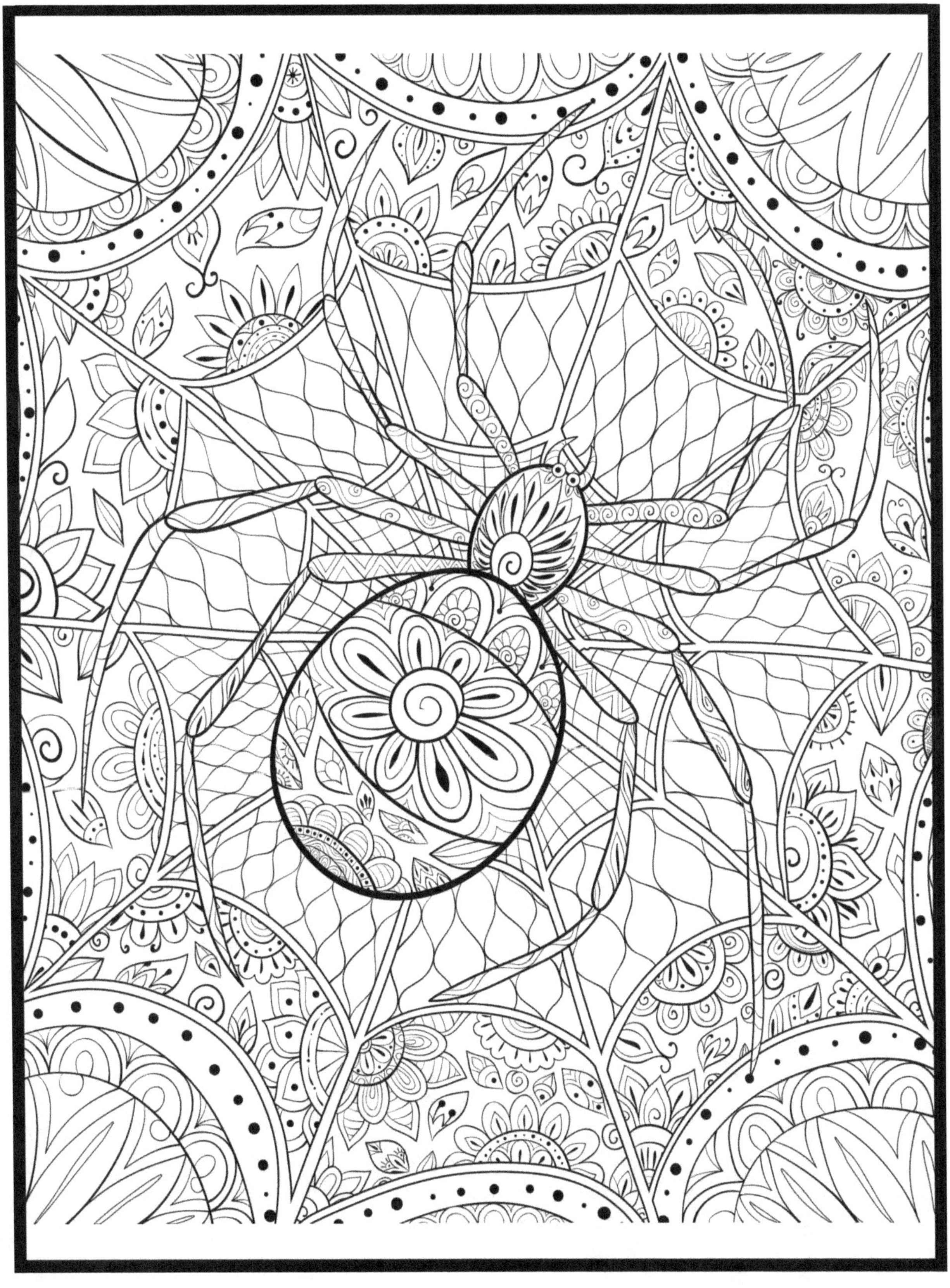

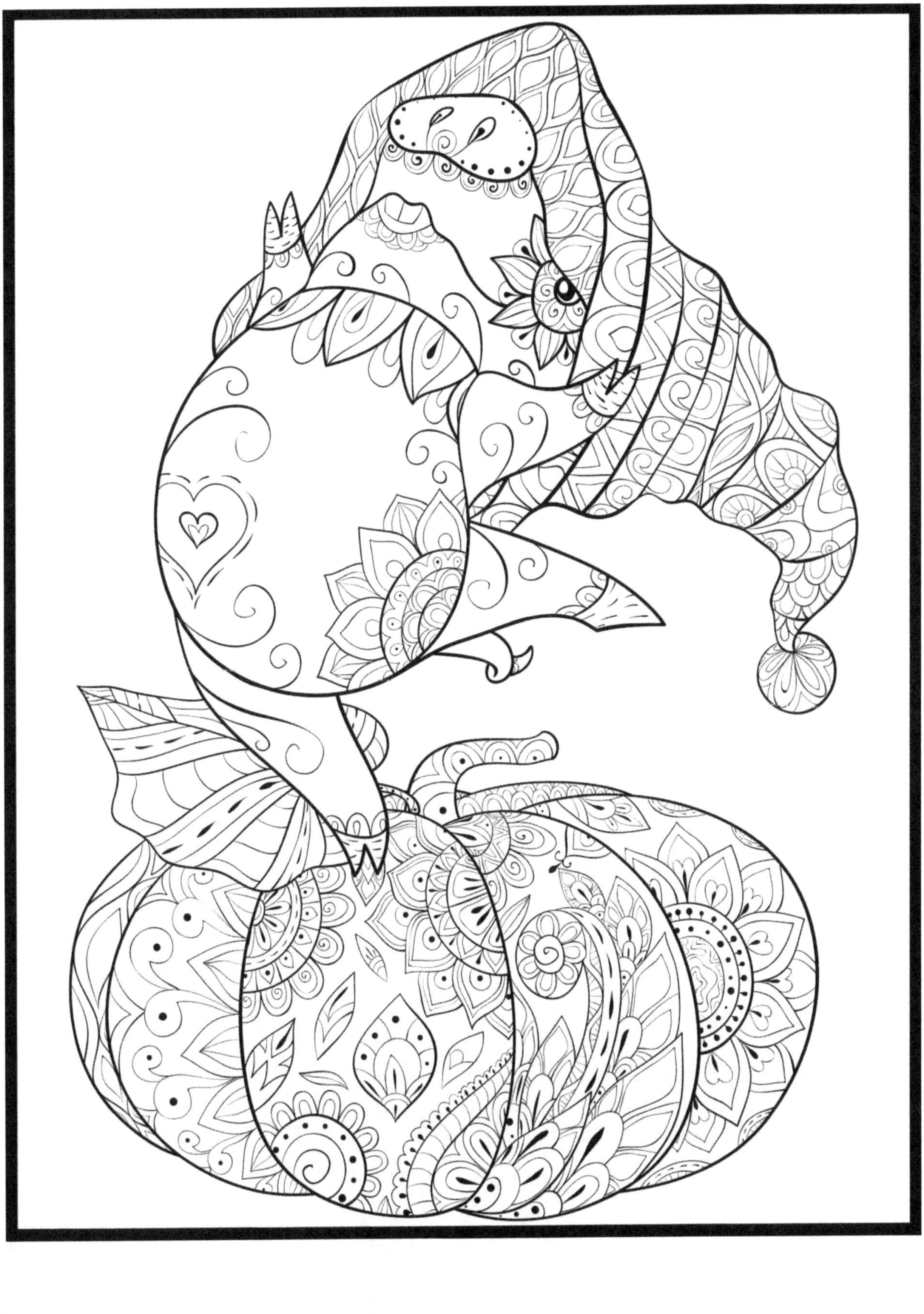

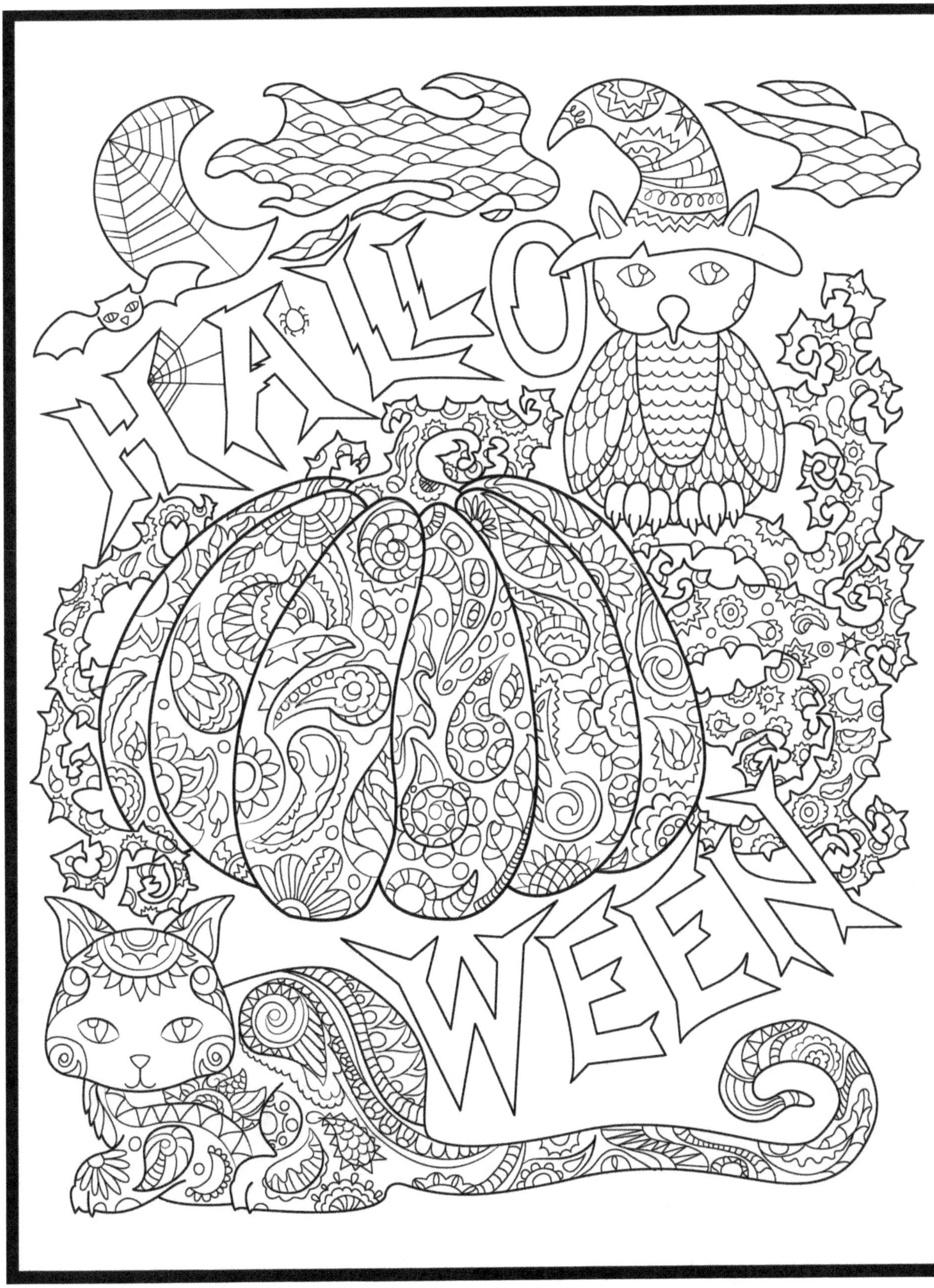
HALLOWEEN

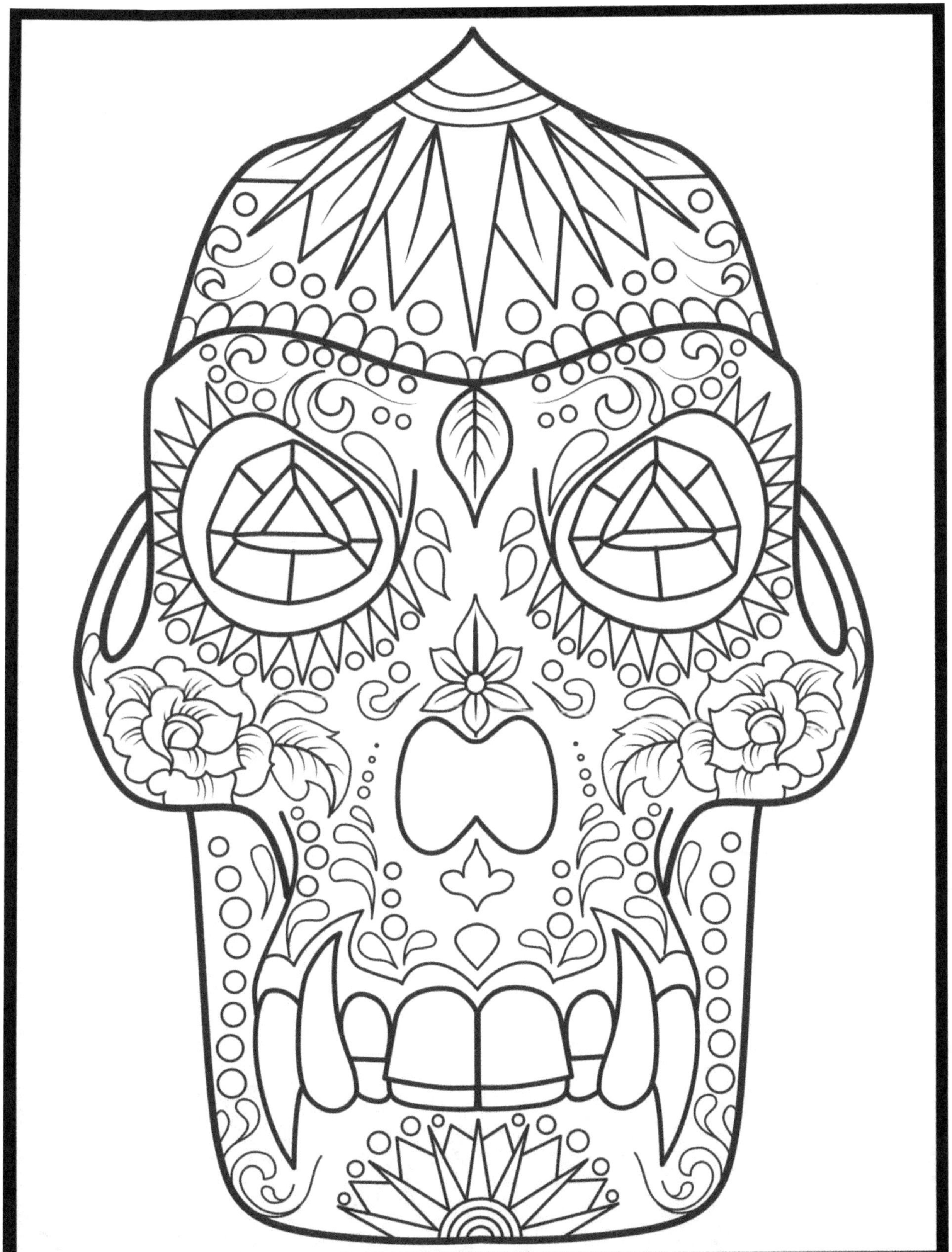

www.ingramcontent.com/pod-product-compliance
Lightning Source LLC
Chambersburg PA
CBHW082252220526
45469CB00009B/2968
9781727072259